Living Through History

RADICALS, RAILWAYS AND REFORM: BRITAIN 1815-51

RICHARD TAMES

B.T. Batsford Ltd London

ACKNOWLEDGMENTS

The Author and Publishers would like to thank the following for their kind permission to reproduce copyright illustrations: Mandel Archive for figures 5, 13, 27, 28, 29, 30, 33, 40, 41, 42, 44, 48 and 51; Mansell Collection for the frontispiece and figures 1, 2, 3, 4, 6, 7, 8, 9, 10, 11, 12, 14, 15, 16, 17, 18, 19, 20, 23, 24, 25, 26, 31, 32, 34, 35, 36, 37, 39, 43, 45, 46, 47, 49, 50, 52, 54, 55, 56 and 57; Mary Evans Picture Library for figures 21, 22 and 59; National Museum of Labour History for figure 5; The Science Museum for figure 38; The Tate Gallery for figure 53. The pictures were researched by Patricia Mandel.

Cover illustrations
The colour illustration shows the Sankey viaduct on the Liverpool and Manchester railway. This great viaduct was the first of its kind in the history of railways. The portrait is of William Cobbett and the black and white illustration is the title page of Henry Mayhew's *The Adventures of Mr. and Mrs. Sandboys*. All three illustrations are reproduced courtesy of the Mansell Collection.

Frontispiece
The first Folkestone train passing the Bletchingley Tunnel, 1843.

Typeset by Tek-Art Ltd, West Wickham, Kent
Printed in Great Britain by
R J Acford
Chichester, Sussex
for the publishers
B.T. Batsford Ltd
4 Fitzhardinge Street
London W1H 0AH

ISBN 0 7134 5264 1

CONTENTS

THE ILLUSTRATIONS

BRITAIN 1815-51

The victory at Waterloo ended almost a quarter century of war. But peace did not bring tranquillity. Orders for military and naval equipment ceased abruptly. The result was unemployment. Hundred of thousands of men were discharged from the armed forces. The result was more unemployment. Unemployment implied disorder. Disorder implied uncertainty. Uncertainty implied change. Change implied reform.

In 1815 many intelligent people believed that Parliament itself was badly in need of reform. The campaign for parliamentary reform had begun back in the 1780s. But the revolution in France had tainted any talk of reform with fears of "Jacobinism" and had wiped it off the political agenda for a generation. But the fall of Napoleon opened the way for the possibility of change – after a decent interval.

Unemployment and the desire for reform between them provoked a range of more or less violent outbursts of popular discontent – "Bread or Blood" riots in East Anglia in 1816,

the fiasco of the "March of the Blanketeers" in the industrial North in 1817, the "Swing" riots throughout southern England in 1830-1 and the Chartist disturbances of 1842 and 1848.

There were alternatives to attempted revolution. The most positive was emigration, which began almost as soon as the wars against the French ended. The usual target was North America. Between 1820 and 1830 some 100,000 people left the British Isles; the Irish potato famine of 1845-6 raised the figure tenfold to pass the million mark. More adventurous spirits found employment in foreign wars – in the liberation of the Spanish colonies of South America, in the struggle for Greek independence from Ottoman rule and in the revolutions of 1830, which changed a dynasty in France, created a new kingdom in Belgium and changed almost nothing in Poland, except for the worse.

Those who stayed in England were scarcely guaranteed a quiet life. During the 1820s and 1830s the new industrial cities of the North reached their maximum rates of growth. In terms of manufacturing output these were years of dramatic, if uneven, expansion. In terms of environmental conditions they were years of almost visible deterioration.

Perhaps the misery of the poor was no worse than it had been before the onset of such rapid industrial growth. But it was concentrated together on a scale never before seen or even imagined. And it was the more striking by contrast with the new wealth of farmers and financiers who had done well out of the long wars.

The awareness of poverty and deprivation was sharpened by the ability to measure it more accurately. The influence of the philosopher Jeremy Bentham gave a great impetus to the "scientific" investigation of social problems. The "Evangelical Revival" in religion gave social concern a new urgency.

1 A contemporary (1843) engraving suggests that the "People's Charter" enjoys massive public support but will have to be literally forced on a reluctant Parliament. John Bull (far right) looks on, amused and approving.

2 The popularity of the Great Exhibition, satirized by the leading engraver of the age, George Cruikshank. This fantasy was in fact the frontispiece to Mayhew's *The Adventures of Mr. & Mrs. Sandboys* (illustrated on the front cover).

3 Workhouses, popularly known as "Bastilles", were particularly hated in the industrial North. Here, rioters distribute 700 loaves looted from the workhouse at Stockport, Lancashire in 1842. They also took £7 in cash.

There was immense enthusiasm for commissions, surveys and reports, for the collection of statistics and the appointment of inspectors. Reformers saw a land blighted by filth, stupidity, stagnation and corruption. What they prescribed was light, learning and efficiency. Cardinal Newman put their creed in clear and ringing terms:

Virtue is the child of Knowledge: Vice of Ignorance; therefore education, periodical literature, railroad travelling, ventilation and the arts of life, when fully carried out, serve to make a population moral and happy.

If it was an age of investigation it was also an age of persuasion, as the urge to democracy demanded that it should be. The opinions of ordinary people were now supposed to matter. Therefore they had to be informed.

Much of that information came from an ever-increasing range of new publications. The most important was probably Cobbett's *Political Register*, which became available for the first time in a cheap edition in 1816. This "Twopenny Trash" reached an estimated circulation of 40,000 copies and many more readers and listeners. Succeeding years saw the establishment of several other influential journals of both general and special interest – *Blackwood's Magazine* (1817), *The Lancet* (1823), *The Spectator* (1828) *Punch* (1841), the *Illustrated London News* (1842) and *The Economist* (1843). There were also major new newspapers – *The Scotsman* (1817), *The Sunday Times* (1822), the *Evening Standard* (1827) and the *News of the World* (1843).

New institutions were established, dedicated to public enlightenment. There were learned societies – the Royal Asiatic Society (1822) for the study of eastern languages and in the same year the Royal Academy of Music, the Royal Zoological Society (1826), the Royal Geographical Society (1830) and the Royal Meteorological Society (1850). And there were institutions whose main purpose was not to accumulate specialized knowledge but to spread it more widely – the Mechanics' Institutes, founded by George Birkbeck in 1823 for the benefit of working men, and Henry Brougham's Society for the Diffusion of Useful Knowledge, established in 1827. Related institutions included the National Gallery (1824), the Public Record Office (1838) and the London Library (1841). The Public Libraries Act of 1850 perhaps marks the largest attempt to bring knowledge to those who could benefit from it.

Formal education took a major step forward with the establishment, by Bentham and others, of University College (1826), the first institution of higher education to admit students regardless of their religious or political views. Together with King's College, founded by the Duke of Wellington and

4 A contemporary cartoon satirizes the blind opposition of landowners to reform. On the right farmers show support for concession rather than repression. On the left rioters wreck a threshing machine, set fire to a barn and threaten a parson with the noose.

others in opposition to the "godless college", this established the core of today's University of London, which celebrated its hundred and fiftieth anniversary in 1986. Equally significant was the establishment in 1850 of the North London Collegiate School, the first modern girls' school to demand high academic standards. A larger number of people, however, benefited more immediately from the first ever government grant for education in 1833 and the establishment of the first ever teachers' training college in 1840.

Literature, too, reflected the social concerns of the age. Dickens dealt with the cruelties of the Poor Law in *Oliver Twist* (1838) and the shortcomings of private schools in *Nicholas Nickleby* (1839). Disraeli's *Sybil* (1845) dealt with poverty and degradation in the new industrial towns, while Mrs Gaskell's *Mary Barton* (1848) and *North and South* (1855) dramatized class conflict in personal terms.

Newspapers and novels made millions more aware of social conditions throughout the nation than they had ever been before. But railways gave them the chance to experience them at first hand. By 1850 all the major cities of Britain were linked together by direct railway routes. Without the railways the Great Exhibition of 1851 would have been impossible. It received no less than 6 million visitors. When the Duke of Wellington had been told in 1830 that 100,000 men would be marching from Birmingham to present a petition for reform he had replied contemptuously: "Where will they get the boots?" Within ten years they could have come by train.

The Duke of Wellington died in 1852 and his death marked the end of an era. A million people lined the streets to watch his funeral. His passing brought a sense of loss but not of anxiety. Victorian Britain looked forward with even more confidence than it had in his hour of glory.

The Iron Duke (1769-1852)

In an age of change the "Iron Duke" stood for continuity. Duty and common-sense were his guiding principles, Crown and country the objects of his loyalty. Though scarcely a pious man, he had a decent respect for the established Church. "Educate men without religion," he is supposed to have said, "and you make them but clever devils." When Wellington died, full of years and honours, *The Times* summarized his career as "one long unclouded day", and Queen Victoria pronounced him "the GREATEST man this country ever produced". Most of her subjects might well have agreed.

Wellington was born Arthur Wesley. The family changed its name to Wellesley while he was still a boy. An Anglo-Irish aristocrat by background, he came from a tradition of command. He learned the art of war in India and made his military reputation in Spain, leading England's only army to eventual victory over Napoleon's most brilliant generals. Wellington was not a brilliant general but he was shrewd and thorough and not easily rattled. He set the seal on his career by defeating Napoleon himself – the first and only time they met in battle. And thus he ended a quarter of a century of European conflict.

But Wellington never romanticized his calling. He acknowledged that Waterloo was a "damned close run thing" and referred to his own troops as "the scum of the earth". In a letter to Lady Frances Shelley he confessed:

It is a bad thing always to be fighting. While in the thick of it I am too much occupied to feel anything; but it is wretched just after. It is quite impossible to think of glory. Both mind and feelings are exhausted. I am wretched even at the moment of victory, and I always say that next to a battle lost, the greatest misery is a battle gained.

Whatever his inner doubts, Wellington had the undoubted power to inspire confidence in the men he led. One officer wrote: "We would

6 Wellington presiding over a celebratory banquet.

rather see his long nose in a fight than a reinforcement of 10,000 men a day." A Private Wheeler put the matter more directly:

If England should ever require her army again, and I should be with it, let me have 'Old Nosey' to command. . . . There are two things we should be certain of. First, we should always be as well supplied with rations as the nature of the service would admit. The second is we should be sure to give the enemy a damned good thrashing. What can a soldier desire more?

Wellington was cool, calculating and courageous. But he was also impatient of fools and contemptuous of visionaries. And these were qualities that were to serve him ill when he turned from soldiering to politics. Accustomed to command, he found it difficult to persuade. His advice to a new Member of Parliament is revealing of his own attitude to the arts of persuasion: "Don't quote Latin; say what you have to say and then sit down."

Wellington's political career overlapped with his military one. Indeed he had sat in Parliament for no less than four boroughs between 1790 and 1809. In 1819 he entered Lord Liverpool's Cabinet as Master-General of the Ordnance, nominally a military office but in fact one which enabled him to undertake high-level diplomatic missions to the Congress of Aix-la-Chapelle and the Congress of Verona. *The Times* was not impressed by the Duke's suitability for such work:

The natural instruments of negotiation do not appertain to his Grace. He can neither persuade the refractory, nor conciliate the reluctant . . .

Wellington remained in the Cabinet until 1827 and not surprisingly attracted to himself some of the popular dislike which the Liverpool government's repressive measures created.

In 1828 Wellington agreed to serve as Prime Minister himself, not out of political ambition – indeed the prospect filled him with distaste – but out of duty. The King's government must be carried on and if no one else could do it he must. Disraeli called Wellington's period of

office "a dictatorship of patriotism". It was distinguished by only one important measure, Catholic Emancipation, which allowed Roman Catholics at last to sit in Parliament and to be eligible for most government offices. It was a measure which many Conservatives had resisted fanatically for a generation and was implemented against strong opposition. But Peel had persuaded Wellington that the step was a political necessity and that it would be less damaging to the constitution in the long run to accept the inevitable. Wellington was always able to cope with reality, however disagreeable he might find it personally.

Apparently no one, however, could persuade the Duke that parliamentary reform was a political necessity and he resigned in 1830 rather than yield to pressure to go forward with it. Indeed he declared:

I am not only not prepared to bring forward any measure of this nature, but I will at once declare that . . . I shall always feel it my duty to resist such measures when proposed by others.

No one could ever accuse Wellington of leaving others in doubt about his opinions. Wellington's public stand against reform was not without its cost. A mob smashed the windows of his London home, Apsley House, and he was threatened with personal violence on several occasions. Returning once from a visit to the Royal Mint he found himself surrounded by a hostile crowd. According to the *Observer* newspaper:

The mob was so dense that the noble Duke was impeded in his progress and narrowly escaped being unhorsed. There were cries of 'Wellington for ever' and several discharged soldiers who had fought with his Grace cheered him loudly. They said they had fought for him at Waterloo and to protect him they would fight by his side that day if necessary.

Wellington remained unshaken, as he explained in a letter to a friend:

Nothing shall induce me to utter a word, either in public or in private, that I don't believe to be true.

Don't be alarmed Gaffer, he's the only man to give these fellows an answer.

7 Wellington had no sympathy with popular movements.

If it is God's will that this great country should be destroyed, and that mankind should be deprived of this last asylum of peace and happiness, let it be so; but as long as I can raise my voice, I will do so against the infatuated madness of the day.

When it came to the rural disorders of 1830-1 the Duke raised his voice with a vengeance in his own county of Hampshire:

I induced the magistrates to put themselves on horseback, each at the head of his own servants and retainers, grooms, huntsmen, game-keepers, armed with horsewhips, pistols, fowling-pieces and what they could get, and to attack in concert, if necessary, or singly, these mobs, disperse them and take and put in confinement those who could not escape. This was done in a spirited manner, in many instances, and it is astonishing to see how soon the country was tranquillised and that in the best way, by the activity and spirit of the gentlemen.

As Lord Shaftesbury was to observe, the Duke was "a hard man".

Wellington did not reconcile himself easily to the fact of reform once it had happened. Entering the reformed Parliament for the first time in 1832 he looked around him and pronounced with characteristic curtness: "[I] never saw so many shocking bad hats in my life."

Serving briefly again as Prime Minister in November and December 1834, Wellington held office as Foreign Secretary into the following year. From 1841 until its fall he served in Peel's Cabinet as Minister without Portfolio and Leader of the House of Lords and also for a while resumed the post of Commander-in-Chief of the army. In Peel's hour of crisis in 1846 he rallied to his side and spoke in favour of the repeal of the Corn Laws. It was a telling intervention because it signalled to the hard-line opposition that repeal, like Catholic Emancipation, was unavoidable.

8 Wellington in the House of Lords. He points to a Militia Bill, symbolizing his continuing (if scarcely progressive) interest in military matters.

9 Wellington's funeral cortège passes through Pall Mall.

In 1848 Wellington undertook almost his last public duty. He was just short of 80 years of age but still the government's choice to be placed in charge of the defence of London in the face of expected Chartist rioting.

As memories of Wellington's opposition to reform faded into the background and he became more a political fixture than a political fact, his popularity recovered. In 1834, to his personal delight, he was elected Chancellor of Oxford University. At the coronation of Queen Victoria in 1837 he was cheered more lustily than the Queen herself. In the closing years of his life he was regarded with the reverence due to a demi-god. Not that he would have cared either way. For, as he had once said of himself, "I like to walk alone."

His death was the occasion of unparalleled national mourning.

RADICALS AND REFORMERS

The reformers of the nineteenth century can be seen as the heirs of two different traditions. On the one hand there were those, like Robert Owen and Edwin Chadwick, who were essentially children of the eighteenth-century Enlightenment; on the other there were people like Thomas Arnold, and Lord Shaftesbury, whose motivation was essentially religious. And then there were individualists like William Cobbett, who belonged to no tradition but their own.

The leading thinkers of the Enlightenment, known as *philosophes* in France, were inspired by Sir Isaac Newton's vision of an orderly universe, its planets and stars moving in endless harmony. Men like Voltaire, Diderot and d'Alembert hoped to improve human societies so that they too would become orderly and harmonious. Sceptics in religion, they were still optimistic about human nature and believed that the eradication of ignorance, poverty, cruelty and superstition would enable the essential goodness of men and women to flourish.

Continental ideas were tainted for the British by their association with the horrors of the French Revolution. But Britain had its own home-grown *philosophes*, like Jeremy Bentham, who inspired Edwin Chadwick, as well as self-educated visionaries, like Robert Owen. The two men present an interesting contrast, for whereas Owen's schemes were wide ranging and covered facets of human affairs as diverse as nursery education and town-planning, Chadwick became single-mindedly obsessed with "sanitary reform", the problem of providing clean water supplies for all. They were alike, however, in the strength of their convictions and their determination to carry them through into action.

In this respect, at least, they resembled those very different reformers who wished to better the lot of their fellows not to realize an abstract vision of a perfect universe but simply as a matter of Christian obligation. They saw evils which they regarded as morally abhorrent in themselves and worked tirelessly to eliminate them. Again we can see the contrast between the general and the particular. Lord Shaftesbury patronized dozens of good causes, from the better treatment of lunatics to the harsher treatment of bad employers. Thomas Arnold focused all his efforts on a moral crusade to transform the education of the nation's social and political elite. Again we see in both a similar certainty of principle and an unswerving devotion of personal energy to its realization. But they looked for their reward not in this world, but in the next.

The widespread movement for social and institutional reform was a response to the strains imposed by the rapid and unexpected changes which accompanied Britain's industrialization. Only gradually was it realized that reform could not be a once-for-all process of readjustment, because only gradually was it realized that industrialization itself had initiated a process of change which was itself unending.

William Cobbett (1763-1835)

William Cobbett was a man with a great love of England and a great love of the English people. And those were about the only consistent things about him. For he could hate as much as love, and there were many things he hated – from tea to taxes. He was a radical and a conservative. He was an angry man and a kindly one. He wrote pamphlets against the revolutionary Tom Paine, and then sentimentally brought his bones back from America to bury them in his native England.

Cobbett was born in 1762 in Farnham, Surrey, then a small market town on the London to Portsmouth road. And it was a chance to visit Portsmouth, where he saw the navy at anchor, that filled him with a sudden desire for travel:

I returned once more to the plough, but I was spoiled for a farmer. I had, before my Portsmouth adventure, never known any other ambition than that of surpassing my brothers in the different labours of the field; but it was quite otherwise now: I sighed for a sight of the world; the little island of Britain seemed too small a compass for me.

Cobbett first went to London, where he worked for a while at Kew Gardens, then, miserably, in a law office. He escaped by joining the army, where he began to educate himself, learning by heart an English grammar while on sentry duty. Between 1784 and 1791 he served in England and in Canada and rose rapidly through the ranks to become sergeant-major of his regiment. He soon came to realize that he was a good deal more able than many of his officers. And later it became obvious that many of his superiors were not only idle and stupid but dishonest as well. When he left the army he tried to bring a case against a number of officers on charges of corruption. But at the last minute he realized that, whatever his own personal qualities, an ex-sergeant major would have little chance of bringing a case successfully against men who held the King's commission.

So he fled to France, where he was appalled by the violence of the revolution, and so finally settled in America. There he lived by teaching and by writing pamphlets against revolutionary ideas under the name "Peter Porcupine", a suitably prickly title for a writer whose chief strength was a passion to denounce whatever he thought wrong in the strongest possible terms. Philadelphia was in favour of revolutionary France, of which Cobbett disapproved. So when he opened a bookshop he made a point of filling it with books, prints and pamphlets calculated to outrage local feeling, such as pictures of

10 A Gillray cartoon shows Cobbett as a sergeant major beating his stupid superior officers until they learn how to drill their men.

George III and of the defeat of an American fleet in the War of Independence. There was never much moderation about Cobbett.

And it was his lack of moderation that led him into a libel suit which almost broke him financially and which forced him back to England. His anti-revolutionary writings in America led the British government to offer him the editorship of a government-backed newspaper. He turned it down and started his own weekly *Political Register*, commenting on current affairs, which he wrote almost single-handed for the next 30 years, thus becoming the single most influential journalist of his day.

In 1804 Cobbett bought a farm at Botley in Hampshire, which he thought "the most delightful village in the world". He soon added to his holdings until he controlled more than 500 acres. He was a good employer and a keen experimenter with progressive farming methods. But it was his writing that paid for his farming, rather than the other way round.

He was never short of a topic to write about, for everywhere he saw England changing under the impact of war and the rapid growth of industry. And most of what Cobbett saw he did not like.

In 1809 Cobbet wrote an article against the flogging of some Ely militia volunteers by German mercenaries. As an ex-soldier himself he had strong views on the subject of military discipline. These strong views cost him two years in Newgate prison, from where he continued to edit the *Political Register*. He also published "Paper against Gold", an attack on the paper money issued by the government to finance the war against France. According to Cobbett it was paper money that made financiers fabulously rich and labourers wretchedly poor.

In 1817, fearing imprisonment at the hands of the repressive government of the day (and also because he was much in debt), Cobbett fled again to America, where he farmed on Long Island and wrote *A Grammar of the English Language*, which was intended to help poor men educate themselves so that they could take a more active part in politics.

Returning to England in 1819 Cobbett stood unsuccessfully for Parliament in 1821 and again in 1826. Despite these failures his influence continued to grow through a torrent of publications: *Cottage Economy*, which contained practical advice on household matters for the poor; *Advice to Young Men*, which was about personal conduct; and, most celebrated of all, *Rural Rides*, an account of the condition of the people and countryside of southern England, based on his own observations.

My object was . . . to see the country; to see the farmers at home, and to see the labourers in the fields; and to see this you must go either on foot or on horseback. . . .

It is fitting that *Rural Rides* should be

11 Cobbett in prison – pensive but pampered. The quill suggests his continuing journalistic activities. The portrait is of John Hampden, a seventeenth-century opponent of governmental tyranny.

Cobbett's best-remembered book, for he hated towns, London above all, and he saw the rural way of life as the best way of life, because it was the natural way of life. As he wrote in the *Political Register* in 1821,

... if the cultivators of the land be not, generally speaking, the most virtuous and most *happy* of mankind, there must be something at work in the community to counteract the operations of nature. This way of life gives the best security for health and strength of body. It does not *teach*, it necessarily produces *early rising;* constant *forethought;* constant *attention;* and *constant care of dumb animals.* The nature and qualities of all living things are known to country boys better than to philosophers.

Cobbett, as a journalist, was a master of invective, and he used his most venomous sarcasm whenever he saw the ways of the town invading the countryside, or to compare the new and the old to the detriment of the new. A newly wealthy Surrey farmer was an ideal target:

Everything about this farm-house was formerly the scene of plain manners and plentiful living. Oak clothes-chests, oak bedsteads, oak chests of drawers, and oak tables to eat on. . . . But all appeared to be in a state of decay and nearly of disuse . . . there was a *parlour.* Aye, and a carpet and bell-pull too! . . . and there was the mahogany table, and the fine chairs, and the fine glass. . . . And there were the decanters, the glasses, the 'dinner-set' of crockery-ware. . . . And I dare say it has been *Squire* Charington and the *Miss* Charingtons; and not plain Master Charington, and his son Hodge, and his daughter, Betty Charington, all of whom this accursed system has, in all likelihood, transmuted into a species of mock gentlefolks, while it has ground the labourers down into real slaves. (*Political Register*)

Cobbett's readers almost certainly agreed with him. Most may have lived in the industrial towns, but many of them had only recently left the land. Cobbett may have exaggerated the wealth of the newly rich or the relative comfort

12 A cartoon of the 1830s shows a ragged labourer dependent on parish handouts.

in which the rural labourer had once lived, but he did not exaggerate the beauty of the English countryside or the appeal of a life regulated by the seasons over a life organized around the steam-engine and the factory-bell.

Cobbett's love of the English countryside and the rural poor was not mere romanticism. He saw a positive value in the tidal wave of rick-burning and rioting which swept across southern England in 1830-1:

... we owe the Reform Bill more to the Country Labourers than to all the rest of the nation put together: because if they had remained quiet under their sufferings; if they had not resolved not to be reduced to potatoes, and if they had not acted as they did . . . Wellington would not have been turned out, Grey would not have come in, the Parliament would have acted on Wellington's insolent declaration, and we should have had no Reform Bill at all; though, in time, we must have had a terrible and violent revolution. . . (*Political Register*)

Cobbett was finally elected to Parliament – ironically as M.P. for the industrial town of

Oldham – in 1832, after the passing of the first Reform Act, which he had done so much to promote through his own writings. But he did not really take to the House of Commons. Indeed, the first words of his maiden speech were: "It seems to me that since I have been sitting here I have heard a great deal of unprofitable discussion." He was too much used to debating on his own terms to learn to follow someone else's rules. But he fought bitterly against the New Poor Law and made a magnificent speech in support of factory reform in 1833. It was fitting that he should

13 "Mr Cobbett relieving the Industrious Labourer". Published in the year of his death this romanticized picture depicts the idyll of rural life as the author of *Rural Rides* seems to have wished to see it.

speak so well against the evil abuses of the new industrial system. For new industries and the slum towns they created were wiping out the old England and the old English way of life that Cobbett loved and celebrated in his writings. He could do nothing to stem the tide of change. But he could denounce it – and never ceased to do so.

Robert Owen (1771-1858)

Robert Owen was rather a bore, but he was an influential bore. He only had a few ideas and he kept on repeating them throughout a long life. But they were ideas which bore much fruit and awakened hope and ambition in the lives of millions. Owen was a successful capitalist who coined the word "socialist" and pioneered new developments in many fields of human welfare, from education to personnel management and from co-operative stores to town-planning.

Owen was born in Newtown,

Montgomeryshire in 1771, the son of a local saddler and postmaster. An eager reader, he was acting as an assistant to his teacher by the age of seven. At ten he was apprenticed to a draper. At 18 he was in the textile business on his own account in Manchester, having borrowed £100 from his brother in London. Within a short while he had become manager of a large mill with 500 staff. He was just 20 years of age. And not only did he show himself to be a capable man of business. He also joined the Literary and Philosophical Society of Manchester and was invited to serve on a local health committee.

Owen next moved to Glasgow, where he took over the giant textile mills at New Lanark, where 2000 people were employed, including 500 "pauper apprentices", orphan children farmed out by local Poor Law authorities. Owen wanted to make a success of the mills but he also wanted

. . . not to be a mere manager . . . but to . . . change the conditions of the people, who were surrounded by circumstances having an injurious influence upon the character of the entire population . . .

As an employer Owen knew that he had enormous power over the lives of his workforce, not only while they were at work but also in their everyday lives. And he intended to use that power to effect.

The previous owner of New Lanark, the wealthy merchant David Dale, had not been a bad employer by the standards of the time. The mills were cleaner and better ventilated than most. And the pauper apprentices were well fed. But most were only five to eight years old and already working around 12 hours a day. Owen changed things quickly, reducing the hours of work and refusing to hire children under ten years of age. He repaired company houses, introduced a system of street cleaning and opened a store selling good-quality food and clothes at fair prices. The profits from the store were ploughed back into the New Lanark community to pay for further public amenities.

The problems facing Owen were moral as well as physical. Theft and drunkenness were commonplace among the adult workers. But he considered that straightforward punishment would not bring about the results he was aiming at:

I had to consider these unfortunately placed people as they really were, the creatures of ignorant and vicious circumstances, who were made to be what they were by the evil conditions which had been made to surround them, and for which alone society, if any party, should be made responsible. And instead of tormenting the individuals, imprisoning and transporting some, hanging others, and keeping the population in a state of constant irrational excitement, I had to change these evil conditions for good ones, and thus . . . to supersede the inferior and bad characters, created by inferior and bad conditions, by superior and good characters, to be created by superior and good conditions.

Owen abolished the extreme forms of exploitation which other mill-owners considered essential for making profits, and not only improved his employees' working and living conditions but raised their wages as well. Many were surprised to discover that Owen's workers became not only healthier and more sober, but also more productive and that profits actually improved. Nevertheless, some of Owen's partners distrusted his concern with social issues and feared that he would involve them in more "needless expense". In 1813 he bought out these men by finding new partners (including the philosopher Jeremy Bentham) who would be content to accept a 5 per cent return on their investment and give him a free hand to use his own methods of management. In the same year Owen set out his views in *A New View of Society: or, Essays on the Principle of the Formation of Human Character.* In this he suggested:

. . . the character of man is, without a single exception, always formed for him; that it may be, and is, chiefly created by his predecessors; that they give him, or may give him, his ideas and habits, which are the powers that govern and direct his conduct. Man therefore never did, nor is it possible he ever can, form his own character.

By 1815 Owen was confident enough of his methods to want to see them enforced nationally by law, so he began to campaign for factory reform. In 1813 he had appealed to other factory managers to take care of their workers as systematically as they took care of their machinery:

Far more attention has been given to perfect the raw materials of wood and metals than those of body and mind. . . . Man, even as an instrument for the creation of wealth, may be greatly improved. . .

In 1815 Owen published another pamphlet, containing his "Observations on the Effect of the Manufacturing System". In this he argued that in the previous 40 years the rise of modern industry had transformed the character of the nation. The outcome had been greater wealth but also greater greed, more trade but also more dishonesty. Unlike Cobbett, however, Owen realized that it was not enough to bewail the loss of a better and simpler way of life. The problem was to find a way to cure present evils and to look for new ways forward.

With regard to factory reform, Owen found a sympathetic ear in Sir Robert Peel, another successful business man and father of the future Prime Minister of that name. Peel had himself secured the passage of the Health and Morals of Apprentices Act in 1802, the first ever law to regulate working conditions in factories. Peel got the House of Commons to appoint a committee of enquiry into factory conditions and Owen himself gave evidence before it. The Factory Act which finally resulted in 1819 was deeply disappointing to him. To conciliate hostile manufacturers, many of Owen's original proposals were dropped – the law applied applied only to cotton mills; the lower age limit for working was fixed at nine rather than ten; and the maximum hours of labour were set at twelve rather than ten. Worst of all, no inspectors were appointed to enforce the act. It was left to local Justices of the Peace, who were either friends of the mill-owners or mill-owners themselves.

A key feature of Owen's thinking was the attention he paid to education. In 1816 he

15 Dancing in a schoolroom at New Lanark. Note the map and "visual aids".

opened Britain's first ever nursery school. At a time when progressive education meant rote-learning by the monitorial system advocated by Joseph Lancaster, Owen emphasized the importance of the teacher's personality, of learning through play and music and dance, and of giving attention to individual children. Owen felt that the best education needed neither prizes nor punishment but rested on the pleasure of learning. Great emphasis was therefore placed on lively teaching methods using pictures, maps, diagrams and objects, stressing discussion rather than dictation.

The hard years after the end of the long wars in 1815 were marked by widespread unemployment, hunger and rioting. It was a time of great political confusion and uncertainty, as the government of the day attempted to head off imagined revolution by real repression. Owen's solution was to put forward a proposal for "villages of unity and co-operation", modelled on his New Lanark experience. These villages would consist of about 1200 persons settled on 1000 – 1500 acres of land. The inhabitants would live in a single, square building, with a common kitchen and dining hall; but each family would have its own centrally heated private apartment and take responsibility for its own children up to the age of three, after which they would be brought up by the community as a whole. Owen believed that these villages could be largely self-supporting and should be founded by local or central government or even by individual philanthropists. What he had originally conceived as a measure for curing unemployment became a blue-print for an entirely new social order.

Cobbett was scathing, as might be expected, towards anything so new-fangled:

This gentleman is for establishing innumerable communities of paupers! Each is to be resident in an *inclosure*, somewhat resembling a barrack; only more extensive. I do not clearly understand whether the sisterhoods and brotherhoods are to form distinct communities. . . . But I perceive they are to be under a very regular discipline, and that wonderful peace, happiness and national benefit are to be the result! (*Political Register*, 1817)

But it was not Cobbett's sarcasm which scotched Owen's visionary scheme. It was

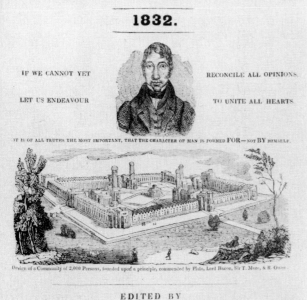

THE CRISIS,

OR THE CHANGE FROM ERROR AND MISERY, TO TRUTH AND HAPPINESS

1832.

IF WE CANNOT YET   RECONCILE ALL OPINIONS,

LET US ENDEAVOUR   TO UNITE ALL HEARTS.

IT IS OF ALL TRUTHS THE MOST IMPORTANT, THAT THE CHARACTER OF MAN IS FORMED FOR—NOT BY himself.

Design of a Community of 2,000 Persons, founded upon a principle, commenced by Plato, Lord Bacon, Sir T. More, & R. Owen

EDITED BY
ROBERT OWEN AND ROBERT DALE OWEN

London

PRINTED AND PUBLISHED BY J. EAMONSON, 15, CHICHESTER PLACE,
GRAY'S INN ROAD,
STRANGE, PATERNOSTER ROW, PURKISS, OLD COMPTON STREET,
AND MAY BE HAD OF ALL BOOKSELLERS.

16 An Owenite publication depicting an ideal community.

Owen himself. For years he had received the homage of distinguished visitors from throughout Britain and overseas. The Duke of Kent, father of the future Queen Victoria, had been vastly impressed by his achievements. But Owen shocked all his wealthy and powerful admirers when he declared openly his belief that all known religions had been founded on error and simply obscured the true path to man's happiness. In an age of religious revival it was not a view calculated to win him allies among the "respectable" classes. But it did little to damage his standing in the eyes of working people, an increasing number of whom were either indifferent to organized religion or actively hostile to it. Owen's ideas about communal property and co-operative living found eager listeners among the poor, who had none of the former and experienced precious little of the latter.

In 1824 Owen went to America to try to put his vision of an ideal community into practice. He bought 30,000 acres of land in Indiana and set out to establish New Harmony. The venture attracted such attention that Owen was twice invited to speak before large audiences of politicians and officials, including President Monroe himself. Owen confidently set out the principles he had practised at New Lanark:

. . . make a man happy and you make him virtuous – this is the whole of my system, to make him happy. . . . I enlighten his mind and occupy his hands, and I have so managed the art of instruction that individuals seek it as an amusement.

Owen attracted a collection of high-minded idealists, restless adventurers and plain cranks. In New Lanark he had found a community ready-made, an unsatisfactory one perhaps, but a community all the same. In New Harmony Owen was faced with the challenge of creating a community out of a very diverse group whose only common feature was a desire to forsake existing forms of society. There were also practical difficulties, such as shortages of building materials and of skilled men to work them. But the critical turning-point was Owen's own announcement that all property should be held in common, that all religions were out-moded and that marriage itself was irrelevant and unnecessary. This was too much even for the avant-garde individualists who had been initially attracted by Owen's Utopia. Some split off to found their own communities. Others were compensated by Owen personally. Robert Dale Owen, Owen's son, explained the failure of the experiment as the result of his father's willingness to accept anyone as a member, regardless of their previous life or character:

A believer in the force of circumstances and of the instinct of self-interest to reform all men, however ignorant or vicious, he admitted into his village all comers, without recommendatory introduction or any examination whatever. This

17 An Owenite "Labour Note".

error was the more fatal, because it is in the nature of any novel experiment, or any putting forth of new views which may tend to revolutionize the opinions or habits of society, to attract to itself . . . waifs and strays from the surrounding society; men and women of crude, ill-considered and extravagant notions. . . (Robert Dale Owen, *Threading My Way*)

Owen withdrew his interest in 1828, having lost £40,000, four-fifths of his fortune. His own rueful conclusion was:

I tried a new course for which I was induced to hope that fifty years of political liberty had prepared the American population . . . but experience proved that the attempt was premature to unite a number of strangers not previously educated for that purpose. . .

Returning to England Owen found that, paradoxically, his influence had greatly increased in his absence. The repeal of the Combination Acts in 1824 had removed a great obstacle to the growth of trade unionism and the growing agitation for parliamentary reform had stimulated an interest in reform of all kinds. Owenite groups and publications were to be found throughout the industrial areas of Britain. Trade union leaders and secretaries of co-operative societies rallied behind Owen in increasing numbers. He addressed the annual conference of the Operative Builders Union, optimistically called the "Builders' Parliament", and drew up plans for the builders to by-pass their employers and take direct control of their industry. In 1832 he established a National Equitable Labour Exchange, with branches in London, Liverpool, Birmingham and Glasgow. At these Exchanges goods were exchanged, not for money but for "labour notes", issued to workers in co-operatives in proportion to the "labour time" represented by what they made.

Disillusionment with the Reform Bill of 1832 brought many more working-class activists into the Owenite movement. This led to an even more ambitious venture, a national "super-union", the Grand National Consolidated Trades Union, which by 1834 was said to have more than half a million members. Another half million were claimed to be enrolled in other unions which supported it. The plan was to organize a general strike as the first step to a peaceful social revolution. But the GNCTU collapsed as its various components became involved in

18 A Cruickshank satire on "New Harmony".

dozens of local disputes, mostly against employers determined to prevent their workers from joining it.

Owen's influence declined rapidly after 1834. Chartism offered a more radical alternative. And Owen himself had nothing new to offer or say. In 1839 he tried again to found another ideal community, Harmony Hall, in Hampshire. It failed. But he continued to write incessantly, repeating his same basic ideas at greater and greater length. In his last years he turned to spiritualism and insisted that he could communicate with the great minds of past ages by means of electricity.

Robert Owen had great qualities – energy, vision and determination. He loved children and was loved by them. His simple ideas spoke tellingly to simple people. But he was also inflexible and often unrealistic. Nevertheless, if many of his projects ended in practical failure his pioneering experiments in education, co-operation, management, planning and labour organization were taken up by others who carried them through to greater success than even he could have dreamed of.

Edwin Chadwick (1800-90)

The British have liked to see themselves as a practical people and have therefore usually thought of philosophy as an abstract, and almost by definition, useless pursuit. But abstract ideas can have very practical consequences, as the influence of Jeremy Bentham shows. Bentham's thinking started from a few general propositions about human nature – for instance that "mankind is ruled by two sovereign masters, pleasure and pain" – and about the nature and purpose of government, that it should aim for "the greatest happiness of the greatest number". Bentham's general approach to existing institutions was to apply a test of utility, to look at a law or an organization and ask "what use is it?". For this reason his followers became known as Utilitarians. They saw themselves as servants of enlightenment, opposed to unthinking tradition and selfish corruption, and in favour of order, logic and efficiency.

Edwin Chadwick was a classic Utilitarian, determined to employ a brisk and business-like approach to solving the social problems of a rapidly changing Britain. Chadwick trained as a lawyer, but never practised law. Living for seven years in one of the poorest parts of London had convinced him that there was other work to be done. His first major employment was to compile the survey of the working of the Poor Law ordered by the reforming Whig government which came to power in 1832. The Report showed that poor relief was administered differently in different parts of the country and argued that payments under the so-called "Speenhamland system", which varied the local level of relief according to the size of families and the price of bread, had the effect of depressing wages and discouraging men from moving to look for work. It proposed that a new Poor Law system should be created, giving uniformity of treatment and providing relief only in specially built workhouses under conditions of "less eligibility" – which meant, in effect, conditions worse than those of any person who could actually support himself from whatever job he could get. It was a case of being cruel to be kind, of forcing men to struggle for their own best interests by denying them any real alternative.

The Poor Law Amendment Act passed into law in 1834 and Chadwick was appointed secretary to the Commissioners who were to bring the new system into operation. He soon became one of the most hated men in the country. Riots against the New Poor Law

19 Edwin Chadwick in 1848.

20 Marylebone workhouse – an overnight ward for the homeless.

were widespread, especially in the industrial North, where many of the new workhouses were burned down.

Chadwick's position as secretary to the Poor Law Commissioners gave him access to numerous statistics and surveys, and from these he compiled a massive, horrifying and highly influential *Report on the Sanitary Condition of the Labouring Population*, which was published in 1842. It revealed that "the annual slaughter in England and Wales from preventible cases of typhus which attacks persons in the vigour of life, appears to be double the amount of what was suffered by the Allied Armies in the battle of Waterloo".

Chadwick summarized the extent of Britain's sanitary problems as follows:

– disease caused by filth was to be found in every part of the kingdom, in village and city alike.
– high wages and an abundant diet offered no protection against epidemic disease.
– young people growing up in insanitary conditions were not only less healthy but more criminal and less able to benefit from education.
– most of the 43,000 widows and 112,000 orphans paid for out of the poor rates were the families of men who had died aged 45 or under as a result of preventible disease.

He proposed the following remedies:

– top priority to be given to the building of proper drains, the organization of efficient refuse collection and the provision of clean water supplies.
– all new public works to be carried out by trained civil engineers, rather than locally appointed amateurs.
– district medical officers to be appointed to propose local improvements and ensure that they were carried out.

Chadwick concluded:

the removal of noxious physical circumstances, and the promotion of civic, household and personal cleanliness, are necessary to the improvement of the moral condition of the population; for that sound morality and refinement in manners and health are not long found co-existent with filthy habits amongst any class of the community.

Chadwick followed up the attack with a supplementary report the following year on *The Practice of Interment in Towns*, which showed that old, overcrowded and insanitary churchyards, where coffins were buried almost literally on top of one another, had become a major cause of pollution in urban water supplies. His main recommendation was that municipal cemeteries, remote from city centres, should be opened.

Further documentation of the hopeless inadequacy of present environmental services was provided in a further *Report on the Sanitary Condition of Large Towns and Populous Districts*, published in 1845. In the same year, however, a scandal was reported in the workhouse at Andover in Hampshire, where the overseer was accused of deliberate cruelty toward the inmates and of embezzling supplies intended for their support. Enquiries revealed that the paupers who were employed in crushing bones (to make glue or fertilizer) had been reduced to eating their gristle and marrow to keep alive. As a result of these investigations the Poor Law Commission was abolished and Chadwick lost his job.

The Public Health Act of 1848, itself largely the outcome of Chadwick's 1842 Report, set up a new General Board of Health, and Chadwick was appointed one of its three members. It was soon put to a severe test, when an outbreak of cholera struck London the following year. Lord Shaftesbury's diary reveals how the Board and its employees responded:

September 7th – Labour and anxiety at Board of Health very great. We are now in the City of the Plague. . . . Disorder increasing, close of last week showed a mortality trebling the average of London; 1,881 victims of this awful scourge! Yesterday showed, for the metropolis alone, a return of 345 in one day . . .
September 9th – London is emptied. . . .

21 A *Punch* cartoon satirizes the germs in London's domestic water supply. But cholera was no joke. Notice that the figure on the right is holding a coffin.

September 17th — We have indeed toiled unceasingly, and not as mere officials, but with earnestness and feeling. Chadwick and Smith are men who may feel, but who know not fatigue . . . when necessity urges or duty calls. As for the staff of the Board, miserably paid as they are. . . . I am unable to speak with adequate praise. They have laboured even to sickness and when struck down by the disease, have hastened back to their work. . .

Chadwick could certainly show zeal and even heroism, but seldom tact. His blunt, aggressive manner and single-minded obsession with "sanitary reform" made him enemies and alienated supporters. The 1848 Act had established the Board of Health for an experimental period of five years. In 1854 its powers were severely limited and in 1858 it was abolished altogether. Chadwick, the champion of central government action, never held an official post again. But he continued to work tirelessly for his chosen cause and in the closing years of his life finally achieved belated public recognition for his efforts, being elected president of the Association of Sanitary Inspectors and being knighted the year before his death.

Looking back it may seem difficult to imagine who could possibly have wanted to oppose what seem to be such eminently sensible reforms. But "great reforms upset great interests". There were, first of all, those who were responsible for providing the established public services. And there were the ratepayers who would have to pay more for the new and better ones. Most of them were better-off than average and believed that the services would be mainly for the benefit of those who were worse off than average. This was an error. Cholera was no respecter of incomes. And Chadwick could prove that they would cost much less than his opponents claimed, that the cost could be spread over many years into the future and that efficient drains and water supplies would in the long run be much cheaper to run. But Chadwick tended to bore or browbeat his opponents rather than persuade them.

Nevertheless, Chadwick received a most handsome tribute from the philosopher John Stuart Mill, who took over from Bentham the leadership of the Utilitarian school:

. . . he is one of the contriving and organizing minds of the age; a class of mind of which there are very few and still fewer who apply those qualities to the practical business of

22 Improving the main sewer in Fleet Street 1845.

government. He is, however, one of the few men I have known who has a passion for the public good; and nearly the whole of his time is devoted to it in one form or another.

The historian G.M. Young also summarized Chadwick's character and career in telling phrases:

Born . . . in a Lancashire farmhouse where the children were washed all over, every day, the mainspring of Chadwick's career seems to have been a desire to wash the people of England all over, every day, by administrative order. . . . Napoleon III once asked him what he thought of his improvements in Paris. "Sir," he answered, "it was said of Augustus that he found Rome brick and left it marble. May it be said of you that you found Paris stinking and left it sweet." It might stand for Chadwick's epitaph. He found England stinking. If he did not leave it sweet, the fault was certainly not his. (G.M. Young, *Victorian England: Portrait of an Age*)

Thomas Arnold (1795-1842)

Thomas Arnold was an unusual man – a great scholar who was also a great educator. When he was himself a schoolboy the great public schools had become notorious for their low academic standards and even lower standards of behaviour. According to the *Westminster Review* the average Eton boy acquired from his exclusive education "a confirmed taste for gluttony and drunkenness, an aptitude for brutal sports and a passion for female society of the most degrading kind". By transforming one such school – Rugby – Arnold, in little more than a decade, provided both a model and an example by which the others could transform themselves. The effect of his reforms long outlived his own early death and revolutionized the training and outlook of England's social and political elite.

The man who was to set the upper classes on a new path was not himself of aristocratic birth but the son of an Isle of Wight customs officer. Educated at Winchester and Oxford, Arnold was an outstanding classical scholar, winning several university prizes and being made a Fellow of Oriel College at the early age of 20. After four years at Oriel and having taken Holy Orders, Arnold devoted himself for nine years to the work of a parish priest and tutored young men for university entrance. In 1828, at the urging of friends, he reluctantly offered himself as a candidate for the vacant post of Master of Rugby School. He had never had any experience of running any kind of organization but, in recommending him for the post, the Provost of Oriel confidently predicted that Arnold "would change the face of education all through the public schools of England". And that was what he proceeded to do.

Arnold had high ideals, but he was also a realist. The father of a large family himself, he had no illusions about the human material he would have to work with. As he wrote to a friend at the time of his appointment:

My object will be, if possible, to form Christian men, for Christian boys I can scarcely hope to make.

Arnold's order of priorities was clear:

What we must look for here is, first, religious and moral principles; secondly, gentlemanly conduct; thirdly, intellectual ability.

It was a revealing order of preferences.

Religion lay at the heart of Arnold's enterprise, and he put the school chapel at the centre of the life of the school. He disliked elaborate services and placed the emphasis in worship on sermons with a clear, strong moral message, usually preached by himself.

Arnold stressed, before all, the formation of "character" as the prime aim of education. And by "character" he meant a compelling sense of duty and moral seriousness. The example of masters would obviously be a major influence on the development of such qualities and he chose his staff with care, appointing young and enthusiastic teachers with a genuine love of learning and a reluctance to use the cane as their normal method of inducing obedience. But example alone would not suffice. Boys also needed to be trained to accept responsibility, so he introduced the prefect system, pioneered elsewhere, to give older boys the task of imposing discipline on their juniors and thereby indirectly upon themselves. Organized games were also encouraged as a healthier outlet for youthful energies than drinking or bullying.

Despite his own brilliance as a classical scholar, Arnold did not believe that an unrelieved diet of Latin and Greek – the normal curriculum of the public school until

23 The Reverened Dr Thomas Arnold, 1839.

that time – was sufficient to stimulate and exert inquiring young minds. New subjects such as French, mathematics and modern history were added to the course of study and the teaching of the classical authors was itself reformed by paying attention to what they wrote as well as to how they wrote it. Scientific subjects, however, he regarded as being of severely limited value. Lecturing to the Rugby Mechanics' Institute Arnold confidently asserted:

Physical science alone can never make a man educated, even the formal sciences (grammar, arithmetic, logic, geometry), valuable as they are with respect to the discipline of the reasoning powers, cannot instruct the judgment; it is only moral and religious knowledge which can accomplish this.

Science might be useful from the viewpoint of national efficiency, but Arnold was less concerned with national efficiency than with personal salvation. Nevertheless, science was included in the Rugby curriculum and this

24 The heart of the school – the chapel at Rugby.

reform alone would have made it unique among the public schools.

Reform had, indeed, become the theme of Arnold's life. In 1835 he wrote to a fellow clergyman:

My love for any place, or person, or institution, is exactly the measure of my desire to reform them; a doctrine which seems to me as natural now, as it seemed strange when I was a child.

By 1841 Arnold felt his work sufficiently complete to accept the post of Regius Professor of Modern History at Oxford in addition to his duties at Rugby. He was delighted to return to his University, the more so as his new post was in the direct gift of the throne. But his joy was short-lived. Arnold died suddenly the following year, leaving uncompleted a major scholarly work on the "History of Rome". Arnold's reforms were almost immediately taken up by newly established schools, such as Cheltenham (1841), Marlborough (1843) and Rossall (1844). These foundations catered largely for

the sons of the newly prosperous middle classes, who wanted to have instilled in their offspring the same style and self-confidence which they took to be the hallmarks of the authentic English gentleman. The reform of the ancient public schools, which had traditionally served the aristocracy, had to wait another generation, until a specially appointed Commission, headed by Lord Clarendon, revealed a horrifying picture of educational sloth and abuse in every one of the nine great schools they investigated – except Rugby itself.

The Arnoldian curriculum, and many other of his practices, were strongly recommended by the Clarendon Report, which acquired the force of law with the passing of the Public Schools Act in 1868. Many grammar schools and private institutions had meanwhile, under the pressure of parental expectations, modelled themselves voluntarily on the Arnold system, spreading his influence far beyond the social elite to the far larger number who aspired to become part of it. Arnold had truly become "the hero of schoolmasters" and his reputation can be judged from the fact that a two-volume edition of his *Life and Letters*

25 Rugby at Rugby.

appeared within two years of his death and was still in print 40 years later, having gone through 12 editions.

The mid-Victorian writer Walter Bagehot summarized Arnold's achievement thus:

Dr. Arnold was almost indisputably an admirable master for a common English boy – the small, apple-eating animal whom we know. He worked, he pounded . . . into the boy a belief, or at any rate a floating, confused conception, that there are great subjects, that there are strange problems, that knowledge has an indefinite value, that life is a serious and solemn thing.

But generations of English schoolboys came to know Dr Thomas Arnold, not through personal experience, but as the kindly and protective but distant and awesome figure who looms in the background of Thomas Hughes' classic novel *Tom Brown's Schooldays*.

Arnold's reforming impulse was, in fact, carried forward after his death by members of his own family. His eldest son, Matthew, became a distinguished poet and critic, and also an influential inspector of schools. His eldest daughter married W.E. Forster, the promoter of that milestone in educational history – the Education Act of 1870, which marked the true beginning of mass education in Britain.

Anthony Ashley Cooper, Earl of Shaftesbury (1801-85)

Many reformers are men and women whose hatred and understanding of social evils come from their own personal suffering. But there are others whose commitment is born of conscience rather than experience. Anthony Ashley Cooper, seventh Earl of Shaftesbury, was such a man.

Educated at Harrow and Oxford, he was elected to Parliament in 1826, being just 25 years of age. A strongly committed Christian, he was not one of those who believed that faith was purely a private matter, to be kept apart from politics. In 1827 he recorded in his diary:

I have decided in my own heart that no one should be Prime Minister of this great country unless deeply imbued with religion; a spirit which will reflect and weigh all propositions, examine each duty, and decide upon the highest; be content to do good in secret, and hold display as a bauble compared with the true interests of God and the kingdom. . .

But he had grave doubts about his own fitness for public life:

April 17, 1827 – Saw Jephson, doctor, of Leamington. He assured me he had never met a person with a more deranged system. Knew by my symptoms that my brain must be sadly loaded; enough to bring on any excess of bad spirits. I have suffered dreadfully for many years with headaches, low spirits and most wearisome sensations, attended by great weakness of limbs. Perhaps I shall improve henceforward.
April 18, 1827 – Entertained yesterday strong

opinion that I ought not to give up public business, or rather the endeavour to qualify myself for it. The State may want me, wretched ass as I am.

Although he opposed the Reform Act of 1832, Shaftesbury – or Lord Ashley as he then was – was an ardent supporter of many of the reforms which the reform of Parliament itself made possible. He played a prominent part in the passage of the important Factory Act of 1833, which not only regulated working hours and conditions but also established inspectors to ensure that the law was enforced. He was also a strong supporter of the anti-slavery movement and made a personal crusade of the movement to end the employment of "climbing boys" by chimney sweeps.

Travelling around the country, he took a keen interest in industrial conditions, though what he saw often pained him. Visiting Liverpool in 1839, he was shocked by its contrasts:

Surveyed the town, admired its buildings, commended its broad streets and wondered at its wealth. Ships . . . and commerce with a vengeance and yet (I thank God for it) there seem to be more churches here than in any town I have seen. . . . Thousands of the dirtiest, worst-clad children I ever saw, throng the streets, presenting a strange inconsistency with the signs of luxury all around. . .

Glasgow, however, he found entirely depressing:

Joined Alison . . . and walked with him through the 'dreadful' parts of this amazing city; it is a small square plot intersected by small alleys, like gutters, crammed with houses, dunghills and human beings; hence arise, he tells me, nine-tenths of the disease, and nine-tenths of the crime in Glasgow; and well it may. Health would be impossible in such a climate. . . . Discontent, malignity, filthy and vicious habits, beastly thoughts and beastly actions must be, and are, the results of such associations.

Such conditions would never improve

26 Shaftesbury exploring conditions in the London slums. The incident is dated 1840 but the picture is at least a generation later.

themselves. *Laissez-faire* was not the answer, but firm government action:

Oh! for a temporary but sharp despotism, which, founding its exercise on an imitation of God, would pass beneficial laws, and compel men against their wills to do wisely.

In 1842 he played the leading part in securing the passage of a Mines Act which banned the employment underground of women or of children under ten years of age. In 1844 he was involved in another Factory Act and, in the same year, in the establishment of the Ragged Schools Union. Ragged schools were intended to bring Christianity to the children of the streets, who were beyond the reach of ordinary schooling. It remained one of his favourite charities and he stayed on as chairman until his death. In 1845 he promoted a Lunacy Act, which provided more human treatment for mental patients. It was an unfashionable cause and one of the first in which he had become involved. Florence Nightingale once remarked rather acidly: "Lord Shaftesbury would have been in a

27 A Ragged school, one of Shaftesbury's favourite causes.

lunatic asylum if he had not devoted himself to reforming lunatic asylums.''

But Lord Shaftesbury cared little for fashion and, though he could be wounded by the opinions of others, he was never deterred. In 1845 he recorded rather wearily in his diary:

The (Anti-Corn Law) League hate me as an aristocrat; the landowners as a Radical; the wealthy of all opinions as a mover of inconvenient principles . . . the High Church think me abominably low, the Low Church some degrees too high. I have no political party . . . the floating men of all sides . . . who dislike what they call a 'saint', join in the hatred, and rejoice in it. Every class is against me. . . . The working people, catching the infection, will go next, and then . . . farewell any hopes of further usefulness.

But there was still much to be done. He was much less concerned with abstract ideas of

28 Ragged school, ragged boy – William Blease of Stockport, *c.* 1865.

political justice than with real and specific social problems and believed that effective reforms were the best way to deal with threats of social disorder. In 1848, that year of revolutions, he observed testily:

The middle classes are content, and so are nineteen-twentieths of the working people; but this will be of no avail against indistinct terrors, ignorant uneasiness and speculative, not social policy. A Sanitary Bill would, in five years, confer more blessing and obliterate more Chartism than universal suffrage in half a century; but the world, when ill at ease, flies always to politics, and omits the statistics of the chimney-corner, where all a man's comfort or discomfort lies.

The following year saw London haunted by cholera, but Shaftesbury felt duty-bound to stay in the capital to attend meetings of the Board of Health. In 1850 he was involved in the passage of yet a further Factory Act. Even in his later years his commitment to social reform remained as strong as ever. He worked for the abolition of the agricultural gangs, which employed young children for long hours in all weathers, and he worked for the early closing of shops, to give assistants time off. Believing passionately in the force of example he was himself a model employer and landlord, and a strict upholder of Sunday observance. Yet, at the end of a long, busy and useful life he could still write:

I cannot bear to leave the world with all the misery in it.

Elizabeth Gaskell (1810-65)

Even after the passing of the Reform Act of 1832 few men had the vote. No women did. Parliament was an exclusively male institution. Only a quite exceptional female personality, like Elizabeth Fry, the Quaker prison reformer, could hope to make an impact on public life. But it was also possible for a woman to confront the social evils of the day without forsaking the approved roles of wife and mother and living quietly at home. By appealing to the imagination and the conscience of a serious-minded age the novelist could hope to influence opinion just as much as the journalist. And few did so more successfully than Elizabeth Gaskell.

Born Elizabeth Stevenson in Chelsea in 1810 she was the daughter of a Unitarian minister who had become a government official. Brought up in Knutsford, Cheshire, she married at the age of 22. Her husband, also a Unitarian minister, worked in the expanding industrial city of Manchester. With her

29 Elizabeth Gaskell (portrait) with various editions of her books and (bottom) a commemorative stamp issued in her honour in 1980.

husband's help and encouragement Mrs Gaskell published her first work, a poem, in *Blackwood's Magazine* in 1837. Its title is revealing of her life-long concern with social issues – "Sketches among the Poor".

In 1844 the Gaskells' only son died of scarlet fever. To distract her from her grief William Gaskell persuaded his wife to begin work on a novel. The result was *Mary Barton: a Tale of Manchester Life*, published in 1848, a year of great social tension as the Chartist agitation reached its climax. The book tells the story of John Barton, an honest working man who becomes an active trade unionist during the hard times of the early 1840s. His daughter Mary is torn between the affections of two men – Jem Wilson, a young engineer, and Henry Carson, her father's wealthy employer. When Henry Carson is murdered suspicion falls inevitably on Jem, although Mary herself knows that in fact the murderer was her own father, chosen to act on behalf of his fellow-workers. And so to Mary falls the fearful task of clearing Jem's name without betraying her parent. . .

Mary Barton was an immediate success. It painted a grim picture of conditions in the textile industry, but was undeniably based on first-hand knowledge. Outraged Lancashire mill-owners denounced it and the London newspapers sided with them. But *Mary Barton* won the firm approval of Thomas Carlyle, the foremost literary critic of the day. Mrs Gaskell had become an instant celebrity with her first book.

Dickens began to publish Elizabeth Gaskell's work regularly in his family magazines *Household Words* and *All the Year Round*. Some of these sketches of local life and customs were collected together and revised to make Mrs Gaskell's second, and perhaps most famous, novel – *Cranford* – which appeared in 1853. *Cranford* is, in fact, the Knutsford of the 1830s, where small town manners and morals were painfully coming to terms with the realities of the new industrial age.

In the same year another new novel by Mrs Gaskell appeared – *Ruth*. Like *Mary Barton* it provoked much controversy, for whereas *Cranford* gently poked fun at small town

30   The stuff of fiction? – Manchester mill workers.

snobbery *Ruth* tells the harrowing story of a "fallen woman"; abandoned by her wealthy lover, she struggles to bring up her son and restore her reputation, only to die in a cholera epidemic, ministering to the man responsible for her fate.

Mrs Gaskell's attempt to win the sympathy of her readers for the thousands of girls who shared Ruth's fate at the hands of so-called Christians was as unwelcome as it was courageous. The novel was publicly burned. Lending libraries withdrew it from their lists. Several of Mrs Gaskell's friends made their personal disapproval quite clear to her. But the praise of Charles Dickens, Charles Kingsley, Charlotte Brontë and Florence Nightingale more than made up for that.

Elizabeth Gaskell returned to the world of *Mary Barton* in her next novel, *North and South*, which contrasted life in the imaginary northern city of Milton, with the easy ways of rural Hampshire. As usual the central character is a spirited and intelligent young woman, Margaret Hale, the daughter of a high-minded vicar. And once again the author skilfully combined a powerful love-story, involving Margaret and the ruthless mill-owner John Thornton, with a dramatic account of industrial strife, this time involving a violent strike.

North and South appeared in 1855 and in the same year Elizabeth Gaskell's good friend

Charlotte Brontë died. Shy Charlotte had written of her in the warmest terms:

She lives in a large, cheerful, airy house, quite out of Manchester smoke; a garden surrounds it, and . . . a whispering of leaves and perfume of flowers always pervades the rooms. Mrs Gaskell herself is a woman of whose conversation and company I should not tire. She seems to me kind, clever, animated and unaffected.

It was appropriate, therefore, that Mrs Gaskell should turn aside from novels for a while to write the *Life of Charlotte Brontë*, which so moved the finest of all Victorian novelists – George Eliot – that she wept as she read it.

Elizabeth Gaskell continued to write until her death, all of her later novels mixing together the familiar ingredients of romantic interest and realistic setting which had first brought her success. A devoted wife and a loving mother of four daughters, she had a generous mind and nature which won the admiration of leading literary figures not only in Britain but also abroad. The celebrated George Sand paid her a tribute which was as handsome as it was perceptive:

Mrs Gaskell has done what neither I nor other female writers in France can accomplish; she has written novels which excite the deepest interest in men of the world, and yet which every girl will be the better for reading.

Thomas Fowell Buxton (1786-1845)

"Good woodcock shooting is a preferable thing to glory." That was the considered opinion of Thomas Fowell Buxton; which is why, perhaps, so few people have heard of him compared with, say, Elizabeth Fry or William Wilberforce. Yet he was the brother-in-law of the former and the tireless ally of the latter and, arguably, as effective a reformer and philanthropist as either. When he died, a memorial to him was erected in Westminster Abbey at the personal initiative of the Prince Consort. Another stands thousands of miles away in Freetown, Sierra Leone.

A brilliant scholar, a model employer and a fervent Christian, Buxton campaigned to relieve suffering among Spitalfields weavers and Newgate prisoners, to end slavery in the West Indies and to spread Christianity in Africa. Yet he was an English countryman at heart, born and bred in Essex and dying in Norfolk.

Buxton was born into a well-connected and public-spirited family. His father, also called

Thomas Fowell Buxton, lived in the village of Earls Colne, near the ancient cloth-working town of Coggeshall, where Buxtons had lived as far back as the reign of Henry VIII. In 1782 he had married Anna, daughter of Osgood Hanbury, of the famous brewing dynasty. (The firm of Truman, Hanbury and Buxton still bears the name of all three allied families.) In 1786, on 1 April, Thomas Fowell Buxton junior was born at Castle Hedingham, a few miles to the west of his family home. His father's career reached its peak in 1789, when he served as High Sheriff for Essex, an office which brought with it responsibility for the welfare of prisoners, for whom Buxton senior appears to have shown unusual concern. He died, however, when his son and heir was but six years old. The formative influences on the young boy's life were to be his formidable mother – a woman of great piety and total certainty, who demanded nothing less from her children than total obedience – and Abraham Plastow, the estate gamekeeper, an

unlettered man but respected throughout the neighbourhood for his upright character. Thanks to them the young Thomas Buxton acquired a profound religious faith and a life-long passion for field-sports of all kinds.

Buxton's formal education began at the tender age of four and a half, when he was sent away to school at Kingston, where he was treated so cruelly that he was soon removed to the school of the celebrated Dr Burney at Greenwich. Burney's teaching must have been outstanding, for when the young man progressed to Trinity College, Dublin, he passed with first class honours in all but one of his 13 examinations and was awarded the university's gold medal. He was also asked if he would like to consider becoming its M.P. He was just 21.

Declining the offer of the university seat, Buxton returned to England to marry into the wealthy and influential Gurneys, a Norwich Quaker family, whose most illustrious member, Elizabeth Fry, was to become Buxton's sister-in-law.

Entering the family brewing business in 1808, Buxton immediately began to take an interest in the welfare of his employees, starting with a simple scheme for educating their children. As his interests broadened he became involved in efforts to relieve the distress of the starving weavers of Spitalfields and at a memorable meeting at the Mansion House spoke with such eloquence that he

31 Riding to hounds, the passion of the country gentry.

raised £43,000 on the spot. From 1816 onwards he gave much support to Mrs Fry's efforts on behalf of prison reform. But his interests widened even further after his entry into Parliament in 1818 as Member for Weymouth, when he became involved in the campaign to end slavery in the British empire.

The trade in slaves had been abolished throughout the British empire back in 1807, but slavery as an institution still survived. The main obstacle to its extinction was the organized opposition of the slave-owners. These men were also property owners and, as such, appealed powerfully to the landed interest on the grounds that freeing the slaves would be an attack on the rights of property, and that an attack on one form of property was an attack on all. Eventually they were to be bought off by a scheme of compensation costing the British taxpayer some £20 million. Victory for the abolitionists came at last in 1834, as Wilberforce lay dying. That it did so was largely thanks to the untiring efforts of Buxton, who had carried the major burden of the struggle for more than a decade. As people remarked at the time, they made an ill-assorted pair; Wilberforce, the "shrimp", five feet tall and in the feeblest of health, and Buxton, nick-named "the Elephant", a strapping John Bull figure, bursting with vigour. But they were united by their Evangelical convictions and a determination to free 800,000 of their fellow beings.

Nor was anti-slavery the only cause to which Buxton devoted his energies in Parliament. Another was reform of the penal code. When Buxton entered the House there were 230 offences carrying the death penalty. When he left there were nine. And much of the credit for this must go to him personally.

The death of William IV in 1837 led to the calling of an election in which Buxton finally lost his seat. He was offered no less than 27 other safe seats to choose from in its place, but he declined them all, though he was pleased to be made a baronet in 1840, once he was sure that none of his friends had suggested the honour on his behalf.

Realizing that it was one thing to free slaves within the British empire and quite another to end the trade outside its territories Buxton pressed for a strengthening of anti-slaving patrols by British warships off the coast of West Africa and supported the organization of an expedition up the River Niger. This carefully prepared venture, which even involved the construction of specially designed modern steam-ships, was intended to spread peaceful trade and the Christian gospel as antidotes to slaving. The ill-fated Niger expedition of 1841 was, however, plagued by tropical illnesses which carried off many of its members and discouraged further enterprise for a decade, though Livingstone was later to pay warm tribute to its pioneering achievements. Saddened by the outcome of the Niger venture, Buxton retired more into private life and devoted himself to improving the estates he had acquired around Cromer in Norfolk. At Runton and Northrepps he created two "model farms" to popularize the most up-to-date farming methods of the day. The remainder of his time he filled with the field sports at which he excelled. When he died in 1845 he was honoured by thousands who had never known him and by all those who had.

32 Thomas Fowell Buxton in 1821, shortly after his election to Parliament.

33 Seal of the Slave Emancipation Society, designed by Josiah Wedgwood.

THE ENGINEERS

Revolutionaries build barricades. Engineers build bridges. But engineers can be revolutionaries, too. And whereas the rebels of 1830 and 1848 aimed to overthrow the tyranny of political despotism, the men who made Britain's railways aimed to conquer two far older tyrants – time and distance.

Until the coming of the railways no man could travel faster than a horse could carry him. In 1851 *The Economist* reckoned that in 1828 the average speed of travel was ten miles an hour

. . . and sensible and scientific men were ready to affirm and eager to prove that this rate could never be materially exceeded; – in 1850 it is habitually forty miles an hour and seventy for those who like it.

Railways made Britain more of a United Kingdom that it had ever been before. Not only was it possible to travel between the nation's great cities in a matter of hours rather than days, but now, thanks to the speed and cheapness of rail transport, it was possible to send printed materials in unprecedented quantities. Without the railways neither the penny post nor national newspapers would have been possible. Without railway timetables the general adoption of Greenwich Mean Time would have been unnecessary.

Railways stood for speed, order and efficiency. They exhilarated Victoria's subjects by what they stood for as much as by what they achieved. Addressing the Institution of Civil Engineers in 1856, its President, Robert Stephenson, reminded his audience that Britain's 8,000 miles of railways

. . . in length . . . exceeded the ten chief rivers of Europe united, and more than enough of single rails were laid to make a belt of iron round the globe . . . they had penetrated the earth with tunnels to the extent of more than fifty miles – there were eleven miles of viaduct in the vicinity

of the metropolis alone . . . 80,000,000 train miles were run annually on the railways. . . . The engines, in a straight line, would extend from London to Chatham; the vehicles from London to Aberdeen . . . the engines consumed annually 20,000,000 tons of coal so that in every minute of time four tons of coal flashed into steam twenty tons of water, an amount sufficient for the supply of the domestic and other wants of the town of Liverpool.

If railways stimulated the imagination they also gave an immense boost to the economy. Stephenson estimated their direct contribution in terms of employment:

90,000 men were employed directly and upwards of 40,000 collaterally; 130,000 men with their wives and families, representing a population of 500,000 souls; so that one in fifty of the entire population might be said to be dependent on railways.

Tens of thousands more were employed in construction and in the industries upon which construction and maintenance depended. According to Stephenson:

20,000 tons of iron required to be replaced annually; and 26,000,000 sleepers annually perished; 300,000 trees were annually felled to make good the loss of sleepers.

Brick-making, iron-founding and engineering were the chief beneficiaries of railway building; but so also were wholesaling and retailing, city centre hotels, sea-side resorts and thousands of shrewd and fortunate investors. The victims were thousands more not so lucky investors and, more visibly, the canal companies and the mail-coaches which simply could not compete in terms of speed, cheapness or reliability. With their decline the slow-paced life of "Merrie England" vanished also.

George Hudson (1800-71)

It has long been said that revolutions devour their own children; that those who make them are frequently broken by them. If this is true of political revolutions it can also be true of economic ones, as the career of George Hudson well illustrates. In his heyday Hudson won the nickname of the "Railway King". He made himself a millionaire, was elected to Parliament and numbered the Prince Consort among his friends. Twenty years later he was imprisoned for debt in the very city of which he once been Lord Mayor.

Hudson was born the son of a farmer in the village of Howsham, near York. Educated at local schools, he was apprenticed to a York draper at the age of 15, worked hard and was rewarded with a partnership. By the age of 27 he was already a prosperous man of business on his own account. Then a distant relative died, leaving him £30,000, which he far-sightedly invested in shares of the projected North Midland Railway. He became active in local politics and in 1833 started a successful local bank. By 1837 he was Lord Mayor of his native city and chairman of the York and North Midland Railway, which opened in 1839, linking the county seat with the new industrial cities of the West Riding.

Hudson's vision broadened with his ambitions. He helped to promote an east coast link to Edinburgh, via Newcastle. In 1843 he brought off a brilliant coup, persuading three separate lines competing for the traffic of Derby to unite into a single Midland Railway Company, of which he naturally became the chairman.

By 1844 all of Britain was in the grip of "railway mania". Hudson led the opposition to the campaign for government control of railway business. And the opposition was successful. Speculation in railway shares could make a man a fortune overnight. Few wanted the state to interfere, least of all Hudson himself. Controlling more than a thousand miles of railway, he possessed both

34 A man of substance – a flattering portrait of George Hudson.

immense managerial power through his position as chairman or director of different railway companies and even greater influence through the force of his reputation as a business genius. He held extravagant parties for the aristocracy at his Knightsbridge home. He bought a great country house in his native Yorkshire. He was appointed Deputy Lieutenant of Durham and in 1845 contested Sunderland successfully against a candidate

35 Railway Mania I – rushing to deliver plans for new railways to the Board of Trade.

THE RAILWAY JUGGERNAUT OF 1845.

36 Railway Mania II – would-be investors worshipping the locomotive "Speculation" with bags of money.

who had the formidable backing of such leading politicians as Cobden and Bright. (*The Times* thought the event so newsworthy that it chartered a special train to bring the result to London; the 305 mile journey took eight hours.) In 1846 Hudson once again served as Lord Mayor of York.

It seemed that nothing could stand in Hudson's way. But he secured his own destruction by using business methods which were at best dubious and at worst downright fraudulent. When the Newcastle and Berwick Railway Company was merged with the Newcastle and North Shields he increased the number of shares in the new company from 42,000 to 56,000, but omitted to record this fact in the company accounts. 10,000 of the new shares went straight into his own pocket and straight out again as he sold them for an estimated £145,000. For a while his reputation protected him from the consequences of his folly. On George Stephenson's advice he bought the Great North of England Railway for far more than it was worth; but the fact that Hudson had bought it immediately raised the value of the shares from £200 to £255 each. Buoyed up by his "Midas touch" Hudson then agreed to rescue the near-bankrupt Eastern Counties Railway. It was beyond his powers to generate traffic in the relatively stagnant agricultural areas through which the railway ran, but he gave a false impression of success for three years by the simple device of paying good dividends, not out of profits but out of capital.

The pace of railway building began to slacken as the obvious major routes between great cities were filled out. Confidence wavered and as 1847 drew to a close the value of railway shares fell rapidly. £78 million was wiped off the value of the ten largest railway companies. Hudson, who now controlled almost a third of the railway network in an empire which stretched from Berwick to London and from Yarmouth to Bristol, was now called on to face the reckoning in a series of angry shareholders' meetings. One by one he was forced to resign his chairmanships. Committees of investigation were appointed in each case. All reported that he owed the various companies large sums of money – an estimated £600,000 in all.

Hudson acknowledge his debts and began

OFF THE RAIL.

37 Hudson derailed, 1849.

former friends raised a subscription of £4800 to buy an annuity for his old age. In 1869 Sunderland, which he had continued to represent until 1859, staged a banquet in his honour "in recognition of his past services to the town".

Hudson deserved some recognition. He had been among the first to grasp the fundamental point that railways should be conceived of as an integrated system, rather than as a random collection of separate and independent lines. And even his embezzlements had served a useful purpose in the end by convincing Victorian investors that some form of government regulation and supervision of the economy was after all desirable. *The Times*, at least, was prepared to be generous in its estimate of his career, characterizing him as "a man who united largeness of view with wonderful speculative courage – the kind of man who leads the world". The railway historian Michael Robbins has likewise seen Hudson's achievement as a positive one:

to arrange to pay them off by instalments. But when he tried to explain away his difficulties in the House of Commons he was heard in dead silence. He opted, therefore, to live abroad most of the time and tried to recover his fortune by involving himself in various continental schemes, but met with no success. In 1865, returning to his native city, he was obliged to serve a three-month sentence in respect of an unpaid debt. But in 1868 his

. . . among the cheerily optimistic or absolutely fraudulent railway promoters of the boom years . . . he, the most powerful of them all, insisted on promoting only those lines that were genuinely meant to be built. . . . Second, he attempted to secure useful amalgamations. . . . Third, he did try to secure economical working. . . . Without Hudson's insistence on these three principles, and his powerful leadership in support of them, the aftermath of 1845 in the railway world would have been chaotic indeed. (M. Robbins, *The Railway Age*)

Robert Stephenson (1803-59)

George Stephenson, the "father of railways" was a self-taught engineer of genius. Blunt, tough and self-confident, he overshadowed his son Robert in the eyes of the public and also of history. But father and son worked well

together in a life-long partnership, which began with George Stephenson's resolution that Robert should have the education that he himself had missed. Robert, therefore, stayed on at school until he was 16, though he read technical books to his father from an early age. Then he was set to gain practical experience of surveying and engineering by working for three years at Killingworth Colliery. Finally he attended a course of science lectures at Edinburgh University. At a time when technical education was in its infancy it was as good a grounding as a young man could hope to get.

Robert Stephenson's first major employment was to work with his father, not merely as an assistant but as a fully-fledged partner, surveying the route for the Stockton

38 Dynasty – George Stephenson (seated) holds his miner's lamp, while looking up at his son Robert, dressed as a miner. In the background an early Stephenson locomotive passes the old family home at Killingworth.

and Darlington railway and then the Liverpool and Manchester railway. Robert's father clearly had great faith in him, for he soon added to his responsibilities by finding the capital to start up the firm of Robert Stephenson and Company, the world's first locomotive works, with its main factory at Forth Street in the Stephensons' native Newcastle.

At this point Robert's career took an unexpected turn as he took up the sudden offer of a three-year tour of duty as a mining engineer in Colombia. Spain's South American colonies had recently fought for their independence with strong British support, and many schemes were being launched in the early 1820s to exploit the continent's fabulous mineral wealth, using the new technology of steam-power. But the Colombian venture came to little as far as Stephenson was concerned – partly because his specially imported gang of Cornish miners proved immensely quarrelsome and partly because it proved virtually impossible to haul specialized mining equipment, imported at great expense from England, overland through jungle pathways and mountain passes from the coast where they were landed to the mountains where they were needed.

Leaving Colombia with little regret Stephenson decided to come home the long way – via America. Shipwrecked near New York, he lost all his money and luggage but, undaunted, borrowed funds and set off to make his way to Montreal, walking most of the 500 miles.

Returning to England at last, Robert Stephenson resumed charge of the Forth Street locomotive works and also accepted the post of engineer to the six-mile long Canterbury and Whitstable railway, which was to provide a passenger service by using a combination of locomotives, stationary hauling engines and inclined planes. At Forth

39 Stephenson's locomotive factory, Forth Street, Newcastle.

Street he set about designing a revolutionary new type of locomotive which would be faster and lighter than all of its predecessors. The result was "The Lancashire Witch", the prototype for the famous "Rocket" which beat all comers at the celebrated Rainhill trials in October 1829. It was a significant 12 months for the young engineer. In the summer of 1829 he had married Fanny Sanderson, the daughter of a City merchant, and in May 1830 he saw the opening of the Canterbury and Whitstable railway, his first major independent project. Four months later the Liverpool and Manchester came into service.

Success brought more work and, in particular, contracts to supervise the construction of three more short railways. The Leicester and Swannington was the most significant of these, involving as it did the construction of a tunnel nearly a mile long. It also led Stephenson to form a new mining company to exploit untapped coal seams discovered in the course of his survey. Over the years this was to prove a highly profitable enterprise.

Stephenson was now ready to undertake his greatest project yet, indeed the greatest construction project, it was said, since the raising of the pyramids in ancient Egypt – the building of a railway from London to Birmingham. During the course of its construction Stephenson claimed to have walked the entire length of the route no less than 15 times, a total of some 1700 miles, the equivalent of Land's End to John O'Groats and back again.

Passing through the Chiltern hills around Tring, the route required the construction of many embankments and cuttings, all painfully carved out of the earth by the muscles of men and horses, assisted by nothing more sophisticated than pulleys and wheelbarrows. The one-and-a-half-mile-long cutting near Blisworth involved shifting more than a million cubic yards of earth at a cost of £220,000, nearly double the original estimate. But the biggest challenge of all was Kilsby tunnel, where underground springs made the soil treacherously unstable. Thirteen engines worked night and day for 19 months to suck

out the liquid sand. The sub-contractor in charge of the project literally died from the strain of work and so Stephenson took personal charge of the 1300 men and 200 horses employed on the task. It took two and a half years to complete and 30 million bricks to line its 7236 feet of length. But the line was finally opened to traffic in September 1838, four years after construction had begun.

This triumph was followed by a period of misfortunes. In 1842 Stephenson's wife died of cancer. He never remarried. Moving house to be nearer his Westminster office, he lost many of his most treasured possessions in a fire. And then a railway company in which he had an interest collapsed and he had to put up £20,000 to re-start if, selling off half his interest in the Forth Street works to raise the money. Then in 1847 one of his bridges at Chester collapsed when an engine came off the rails and plunged to disaster, killing six people. An official enquiry cleared Stephenson of any responsibility but he did blame himself and never used that particular design again.

Stephenson's next years were largely occupied in building some of the most spectacular bridges in Britain: a tubular bridge across the river Conway in north Wales, opened in 1848; the High Level Bridge across the Tyne at Newcastle, opened by

40 The Britannia Bridge over the Menai Straits.

Queen Victoria in 1849; the Britannia Tubular Bridge across the Menai Straits and the Royal Border Bridge at Berwick on Tweed, both opened in 1850. In *Victorian Engineering* the engineering historian L.T.C. Rolt classified the Britannia Bridge as a work of genius:

Whether this bridge is judged by its advance on what had gone before, or by its influence on future engineering practice, it must undoubtedly rank as the greatest and boldest civil engineering feat of the early Victorian era.

When the British government was asked in 1985 to choose a list of outstanding buildings to qualify for the protection of the World Heritage Convention, the Britannia Bridge was chosen to rank alongside Durham Cathedral and the Tower of London.

41 The Victoria Bridge, Montreal, crossing the St Lawrence where it is nearly 1¾ miles wide.

Stephenson extended his operations overseas, building Norway's first railway line, and constructing two tubular bridges in Egypt and another across the St Lawrence River in Canada.

Robert Stephenson was a great engineer and was recognized as such by his contemporaries, who elected him President of the Institute of Mechanical Engineers. It was an honour he was pleased to accept. The King of Norway invested him with the Order of St Olaf. But he turned down a knighthood. Stephenson was the first engineer to become a millionaire. He used his wealth to entertain his friends and to collect works of art. He also undertook various public duties. Serving as M.P. for Whitby from 1847 he made his maiden speech in the House of Commons in support of the Great Exhibition. Later he served as one of the Commissioners who helped to organize it.

Stephenson died in 1859 at the early age of 56. Despite living in his father's shadow for most of his life, his extraordinary contributions to the nation's progress were recognized by the extraordinary respects paid to him on the occasion of his funeral, which provoked mourning on a scale unseen since the passing of the Duke of Wellington. All the shipping in the Thames flew its flags at half mast. In Newcastle all business was suspended for the entire day. By special permission of the Queen the funeral procession was allowed to pass through Hyde Park, where the route was lined with silent crowds. And finally the body was laid to rest in Westminster Abbey, beside that of another great engineer, Thomas Telford.

Isambard Kingdom Brunel (1803-59)

By his death the greatest of England's engineers was lost, the man with the greatest originality of thought and power of execution, bold in his plans, but right. The commercial world thought him extravagant; but although he was so, things are not done by those who sit down and count the cost of every thought and act.

Such was the verdict of Daniel Gooch, the celebrated locomotive designer, on Isambard

Kingdom Brunel, a restless genius, whose ships were wonders of their age and whose railways and bridges are in service still.

Brunel was born in 1803, the son of Marc Brunel, a distinguished French engineer, who had fled from the revolution to exile in England. Schooled at the Lycée Henri Quatre in Paris and in the engineering workshops of Maudslay, Sons and Field in London, Isambard received the best theoretical and practical training his father could arrange for him. His first professional assignment was to assist his father in building the first-ever tunnel under the river Thames. It proved to be nearly his last professional assignment. In May 1827 a section of the tunnel workings was breached and a massive wall of water swept through. Brunel got his crew out safely and then went back himself to rescue one navvy who had been knocked out. But when disaster struck again in January 1828 the young engineer was not so lucky and himself had to be rescued, suffering a badly smashed leg in the process. Work on the tunnel ended for seven years; and by then Brunel had other projects to occupy him.

But first there were years of frustration. Brunel had immense ambitions and longed to "be rich, have a house built . . . be the first engineer and an example for future ones". But he feared that he would be just "a mediocre success – an engineer sometimes employed, sometimes not – £200 or £300 a year and that uncertain". In fact he seldom lacked work, though most of his projects at that time were unspectacular, if useful, works, like docks and drainage systems. It was a good apprenticeship but he still dreamed of greater things. Riding on the newly opened Liverpool and Manchester railway he wrote:

I record this specimen of the shaking of the Manchester railway. The time is not far off when we shall be able to take our coffee and write while going noiselessly and smoothly at 45 m.p.h. – let me try.

Brunel's first breakthrough to fame came with a competition to design a bridge to span the Avon gorge at Bristol. Brunel's design was the eventual winner, although work did not start on it until 1835 and was not completed until 1864, five years after its designer's death. But the aborted project did bring Brunel into contact with the promoters of a new railway which was to run from Bristol to London. Brunel, just 30, was appointed engineer at a handsome salary of £2000 a year. The G.W.R., the Great Western Railway – God's Wonderful Railway as it came to be called – is his single-handed achievement. The work was finished in 1841 at a cost of £6½ million, more than double the original estimate; but it was, without doubt, "the finest work in England", in Brunel's own words. And in 1842 the Queen herself gave it her personal approval, travelling from Paddington to Slough on her way to Windsor Castle. It was the first time a British monarch had travelled by train.

By the time the G.W.R. was opened to traffic Brunel's career had already entered a new phase – ship design. Until that time it had been generally held among engineers that "steam cannot do for distant navigation". Steam-ships were thought to be useful as coasters and ferries, because they were more reliable than sailing ships. But it was regarded as impossible to design a ship which could carry enough fuel for a long ocean voyage. Engineers reasoned that any ship big enough to carry enough fuel would be too big for its engines to drive along. And bigger engines would mean more fuel and so the same problem on a bigger scale. Brunel, however, saw that increasing the volume of a ship did not necessarily increase its surface area in the same direct proportion. In other words, one would not necessarily need double the power to drive a ship double the size.

Convinced that a transatlantic steam-ship was a practical possibility, Brunel set about convincing others and won the backing of some of the promoters of the G.W.R. The result was the *Great Western*. On its maiden voyage to New York it made the crossing in 15 days – three times as fast as a sailing ship – and with 200 tons of coal to spare.

Before the *Great Western* had even completed her second voyage Brunel was planning to build an even larger ship. In 1843 the *Great Britain* was launched by the Prince Consort himself. It was the world's first all-iron, all-steam-powered ocean-going ship and Brunel modestly called her "the finest ship in the world". But it took three years to complete fitting out and on her maiden voyage in 1846 she was driven ashore by a horrendous storm on the coast of Ireland. The disaster bankrupted the Great Western Steamship Company but the ship itself was reclaimed and spent the next 23 years running to and from Australia. Eventually she was beached in the Falkland Islands as a storage hulk for coal. In 1970 the *Great Britain* was finally rescued from obscurity, towed back to her native Bristol and lovingly restored as a museum to celebrate the achievements of her maker.

Brunel's fame and creative talent threatened to divert his energies into a dozen different tasks. Throughout the 1840s he experimented with an "atmospheric railway" to be run by compressed air. The theory was sound enough but the technology of the day made it impossible to put it into practice. In the end, despite successful trials, the project was abandoned and the equipment sold off at an immense loss to the backers of the scheme. The pumping machinery alone fetched £40,000. More successful ventures included Brunel's service as a member of various committees involved in organizing the Great Exhibition of 1851 and his ingenious design for a prefabricated hospital for use in the Crimean War.

Brunel's later life was, however, consumed by two major projects – the construction of a railway bridge over the river Tamar, to the west of Plymouth, and the building of the largest ship ever attempted, the ill-fated *Great Eastern*.

Brunel had to bridge the Tamar at a point where it was 1100 feet wide and 70 feet deep. His plan first involved the building of a masonry column 35 feet thick in the middle of the river. This would bear the massive 1000-ton trusses which would carry the actual track. On 1 September 1857 Brunel, before an enormous crowd, supervised the army of workmen needed to float the first truss into position and then hoist it up to its final resting place. An eye-witness described the tension of the final moments:

Not a voice was heard . . . as by some mysterious agency the tube and rail, borne on the pontoons, travelling to their resting-place . . . it *slid*, as it were, into its position . . . without any extraordinary mechanical effort, without a 'misfit', to the eighth of an inch.

It was Brunel's greatest hour of triumph.

He would need a success to sustain him, for the *Great Eastern* was proving a sore trial. The basic idea was as simple as it was staggering – to build a ship big enough to take Britain's entire annual exports to the East. Brunel's commitment was absolute:

I never embarked in any one thing to which I have so entirely devoted myself, and to which I have devoted so much time, thought and labour, on the success of which I have staked so much reputation and to which I have so largely committed myself and those who were disposed to place faith in me.

Brunel's determination, however, soon foundered on a complete break-down of collaboration with his partner, John Scott Russell, reputedly the most brilliant marine engineer of the day. Lengthy negotiations were required to buy out Russell and it was not until November 1857 that a first attempt was made to launch the 12,000-ton hull sideways into the river Thames. Six more attempts were made over the course of the next month but the ship had settled so heavily into the mud of

42 From *Great Western* to *Great Eastern*. Bigger – and better?

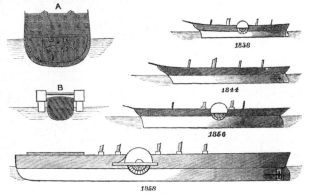

A

B

1838

1844

1856

1858

43 The Royal Albert Bridge, Saltash.

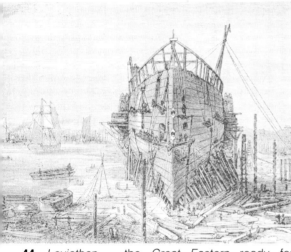

44 *Leviathan* – the *Great Eastern* ready for launching.

45 Partners? Scott Russell (first left) and Brunel (third from left).

the river bank that it burst the hydraulic rams lined up to shift it. Three more attempts were needed, the final one lasting 60 hours. On 31 January 1858 the ship – then called *Leviathan* – was afloat. But Brunel was a broken man.

Travelling the Mediterranean to restore his health, Brunel spent Christmas 1858 in Cairo with his old friend Robert Stephenson. When he returned to England he found that the directors of the new Great Ship Company, which had taken over from the original and now bankrupted Eastern Steam Company, had given the contract for fitting out the *Great Eastern* to – John Scott Russell. Undeterred, Brunel summoned his last reserves of energy, ignored his doctors and pledged himself to put the ship into service. On 5 September 1859 he was carried from the yard, paralyzed by a stroke. On the 9 September the *Great Eastern* set out on its proving trials. Catastrophe struck when an unchecked boiler exploded, wrecked the central saloon and blew a funnel into the air. The ship's brilliant cellular design confined the effects of the explosion and not one passenger was harmed; though numbers of the crew were hideously scalded to death. For Brunel it was the final blow. He died on 15 September.

Joseph Paxton (1803-65)

Joseph Paxton's life was a classic Victorian success story. It showed how a poor boy with no education could become an author, an architect, a Member of Parliament and a very rich man; providing, of course, that he had extraordinary talents and a colossal appetite for work.

Joseph Paxton was born in the small Bedfordshire village of Milton Bryan in 1803. His first job was as a garden boy and he soon showed himself to be bright, hard-working and eager for responsibility. By the age of 20 he was working in West London in the newly established gardens of the Horticultural Society, next door to Chiswick House, one of the many homes of the sixth Duke of Devonshire. The Duke was a shy and restless man whose deafness made it difficult for him to make friends easily and kept him out of politics. Strolling in the Horticultural Society's gardens he often stopped to chat to the business-like young man at work there. One day the head gardener at his great Derbyshire mansion, Chatsworth, retired. The Duke offered Paxton the job. He was just 23; and he needed no second invitation:

. . . arrived at Chatsworth at 4.30 a.m. . . . As no person was to be seen at that early hour, I got over the greenhouse gate . . . explored the pleasure grounds and looked round the outside of the house. I then went down to the kitchen gardens, scaled the outside wall and saw the whole of the place, set the men to work there at six o'clock; then returned to Chatsworth and got Thomas Weldon to play me the water works and afterwards went to breakfast with . . . Mrs Gregory and her niece. The latter fell in love with me and I with her, and thus completed my first morning's work at Chatsworth before 9 o'clock.

The housekeeper's niece was Sarah Bown and Paxton married her in January 1827. She was to bear him six daughters and a son and to play a major part in organizing his career. As the child of a successful farmer she also brought with her a dowry of £5000 – a fabulous sum set beside Paxton's salary of £70 a year.

As head gardener, and from 1829 head forester as well, Paxton brought efficiency and flair to a wide range of tasks – laying out new gardens to set off Chatsworth's newly built north wing; establishing a "pinetum", a special plantation of every kind of pine tree; and experimenting with new designs of glass-

houses. By 1831 he was ready to put his knowledge into print, starting a new monthly magazine called the *Horticultural Register*.

Over the next ten years his career broadened in every direction. In 1834 he brought out the first number of *Paxton's Magazine of Botany*, with beautiful colour pictures. In 1835 he created an arboretum, a collection of every kind of tree available. In the same year he took advantage of his growing personal prosperity to invest in his first railway shares. In 1836 he began work on the Great Conservatory at Chatsworth. Drawing on the results of his earlier experiments, he built in a novel and distinctive "ridge and furrow" style which set the glass as nearly as possible at right angles to the sun's rays, thus minimizing deflection and maximizing heat. Completed in 1840 the Great Conservatory was the largest glass building in the world at that time – 277 feet long, 123 feet broad and 67 feet high, with a central path wide enough to drive a horse and carriage down.

Between 1838 and 1842 Paxton supervised an extensive building programme in the village of Edensor, where the Duke owned many of the cottages. During the same years he published *A Practical Treatise on the Cultivation of the Dahlia* (which was translated into several European languages), a *Pocket Botanical Dictionary* and the first issue of the *Gardener's Chronicle*, which continues to this day. He also travelled extensively on the

46 The Great Chatsworth Conservatory, 1844, described by the *Illustrated London News* as "this splendid pile".

Continent with the Duke, visiting Switzerland, Italy, Greece and Constantinople. And with the Duke's encouragement he began to take on a wide variety of outside jobs – laying out Prince's Park in Liverpool in 1842, then Birkenhead Park in 1843-4 and a new cemetery at Coventry in 1845. Not that he neglected Chatsworth. In 1840 he organized the moving of a 12-ton palm tree from Walton-on-Thames to take pride of place in the Chatsworth arboretum. In 1842 he designed a spectacular rockery and waterfall. In 1843 he devised brilliant illumination to mark a visit by Queen Victoria and the Duke of Wellington. The old soldier was much impressed by Paxton's efficiency in organizing his army of gardeners and remarked to the Duke "I should have liked that man of yours for one of my generals." In 1844 another royal visit was scheduled, from Tsar Nicholas I of Russia. Paxton designed Chatsworth's Emperor Fountain in his honour. On the moors above the house workmen excavated 100,000 cubic feet of earth to make a reservoir big enough to provide the head of water needed to drive a spout 290 feet in the air. Unfortunately the Tsar was too busy ever to come and see it.

Paxton's business interests continued to flourish. In 1845 he was one of four partners to launch a new national newspaper, the *Daily News*. Paxton put up the largest share – £25,000. Thanks to Sarah's careful management of their finances the Paxtons survived the railway share crash of 1845 without loss. In 1848 Joseph became a director of the Midland Railway, which added George Hudson to a circle of business acquaintances which already included Thomas Brassey, Robert Stephenson and Charles Dickens.

In 1849 Paxton found a new challenge – in a water-lily. The plant – then called *Victoria regina*, now *Victoria amazonica* – had been discovered in 1836 in Brazil, where it grew to an immense size. In 1846 seeds of the giant water-lily were brought to Kew Gardens, where they refused to grow beyond a few inches. Three years later the Director at Kew sent one of these small plants to Chatsworth, where Paxton built a special tank which, by means of ingenious lighting and heating, simulated the atmosphere of the Amazon. The water-lily grew and grew until the leaves were 3½ feet across. Paxton enlarged the tank; within a month the leaf was 4½ feet across.

Within another month the lily was in flower, the first to do so in England; and it was big enough to hold the weight of Paxton's seven-year-old daughter. Paxton went to Windsor to present the Queen with a bud and a leaf; then returned to Chatsworth to build a splendid new Lily House to show off his exotic triumph. It was altogether a curious accomplishment. But it proved to be a fitting preparation for the greatest challenge of all.

In January 1850 a Royal Commission was appointed to organize a "Great Exhibition of the Works of All Nations". An exhibition needed a hall to house the exhibits. Designs were called for by a Building Committee which included Brunel and Robert Stephenson. Two hundred and forty-five designs were submitted. But none, in the opinion of the Building Committee, could be built quickly or cheaply enough. By July it looked as though the whole vast enterprise might simply fizzle out, for want of a suitable

47 Building the Crystal Palace. Note the use of standardized constructional units.

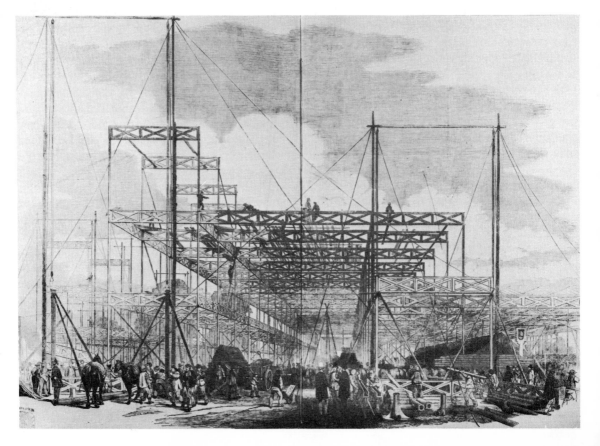

building. Paxton then submitted a design which he had first scribbled out on a blotting pad during a railway directors' meeting. Based on the Chatsworth Lily House, it was checked out for soundness by the chief engineer of the Midland Railway. By the time Paxton's design, with some alterations, was approved there were just nine months to translate a drawing into a building. One man had confidence in Paxton, the Duke of Wellington, who said "It will be ready. I know it will – Paxton has said it will."

Through his connection with the railways Paxton knew enough about modern mass-production to be able to incorporate its possibilities into his design. Fox and Henderson, the railway equipment manufacturers, would supply 3300 standardized iron columns and 2300 girders, which would then be bolted together and assembled on the Hyde Park site chosen for the Exhibition. Wooden roof timbers would be cut to standard lengths by machine. And 300,000 standard size sheets of glass would be put in place by teams of glaziers working from 76 specially designed trolleys running along the gutters. Meanwhile 500 more men would swarm over the building to complete the stunning effect of the glass and iron wonder by painting it all in bold primary colours.

In six months it stood complete – 1848 feet long, 408 feet wide and 108 feet high – three times the size of St Paul's Cathedral and covering an area of 19 acres. *Punch* magazine christened it the "Crystal Palace" and the Queen knighted its creator in October 1851, just as the Exhibition closed.

It had been agreed from the outset that whatever structure was built to house the Great Exhibition it would only be temporary. The Crystal Palace had had its hour of glory and now had to come down. And then? Paxton had a plan and formed a company to buy the building. It was taken to pieces and, with a number of enlargements, re-erected in the grounds of Penge Place, a large country house at Sydenham, then on the south-east fringes of London. Here it served not merely as an exhibition hall, but as what would nowadays be called a leisure centre, staging every sort of

48 Interior of the Crystal Palace at Sydenham.

event from concerts to firework displays. Despite financial difficulties it survived until destroyed by fire in 1936.

The fame of the Crystal Palace brought Paxton many new commissions – to build a great country house at Mentmore in Buckinghamshire for Baron Mayer Rothschild and others near Paris and Geneva for other members of that wealthy banking family; to design Queen's Park and Kelvingrove Park in Glasgow; and to extend the Spa buildings and grounds at Scarborough.

In 1854 Paxton became M.P. for Coventry. Though never a great debater he was an effective committee member and diligent in looking after constituency matters. He was re-elected in 1857 and again in 1859. In 1855 he put forward his most visionary scheme – for an immense glass and iron arcade, 11½ miles long, which would encircle central London, sheltering both a road and a railway and being lined with shops and offices. Nothing came of this amazing idea. But, more practically, Paxton did promote the Act of Parliament which led to the embankment of the Thames and the beginnings of London's modern sewerage system.

Paxton's last years were like those of many successful businessmen. He became almost obsessed with doing business, of whatever kind. Travelling long distances, working long hours, eating and drinking too well, he damaged his health and grew distant from his wife. Her constant letters reproached him for his absences and the loss of their comfortable, intimate home life. But nothing could induce him to slow down. By 1865 his high-pressure life-style had caught up with him. Retiring from Parliament in the spring, he died in June of that year.

Paxton's parks at Liverpool and Birkenhead survive much as he intended them to be. But the Crystal Palace has gone, as have the Great Conservatory and Lily House at Chatsworth. Nearby, however, in the churchyard at Edensor lies the imposing tomb of "Joseph Paxton, Architect", an impressive monument for a village garden boy, whom *The Times* in its obituary described as:

. . . the greatest gardener of his time, the founder of a new style of architecture and a man of genius who devoted it to objects in the highest and noblest sense popular.

LIVES OF STRUGGLE

As Britain adjusted to the impact of industrialism some people struggled for a cause, others struggled to get on and most struggled to survive. It was an age of uncertainty, of possibility and insecurity. The traditional hazards of life – accident, crime and disease – persisted and took on new and more vicious forms in the slum cities of the expanding industrial regions. At the same time, unprecedented and continuing – if not strictly continuous – economic expansion opened up the path to wealth for the fortunate few and to respectability for their diligent dependants.

History itself seemed to have decided to travel by train as everything rushed onward into the unknown future, faster and grander than ever before. Little wonder that millions sought for lost certainties in religion or the promise of a better future in Chartism or emigration.

The increasing activity of the state and the positive explosion of printing and publishing which accompanied the onset of industrialization has left the historian more information about the period than is available for any previous age. With the coming of the decennial census in 1801 and the registration of births, deaths and marriages from 1836 onwards, the raw data becomes available to reconstruct the framework of family life, its joys and sorrows, its crises and rhythms. With the coming of Cobbett's "Twopenny Trash" we see the birth of a mass-readership for political news and with the coming of Chartism the birth of mass-involvement in a political movement that required of its members more than a willingness to riot occasionally and promised more than the relief of particular grievances or traditional hardships. Neither Cobbett nor Chartism could claim much in the way of consistency, but consistency of thought and action is the product of calm consideration and it was a time for urgent action rather than for cool reflection, an age of pamphleteers rather than of philosophers.

We still know little about how ordinary people *reacted* to these changes, what they felt or thought. Despite the efforts of religious charities and enlightened employers only a minority of adults could both read and write or were called upon by the circumstances of their lives to do so habitually. Deprived of literacy they could not cross the gulf of time to speak to future generations. Their voice died with their voices. Only the exceptional set down the record of their lives in any generation. Of the tens of millions who lived and died in Britain between Waterloo and the Great Exhibition no more than a few hundred have left behind them a personal account of the great and little experiences of their lives. The examples that follow may or may not be typical of thousands of others. All that we do know is that by the very fact of their recording and survival they are worthy of our attention and respect.

James Dawson Burn (*c.* 1800-*c.* 85)

Few lives can better illustrate the turbulent condition of nineteenth-century Britain than that of James Dawson Burn. And Burn knew it himself, for when he published an account of his life in 1855 he called it "The Autobiography of a Beggar Boy, in which will be found related the numerous trials, hard struggles and vicissitudes of a strangely chequered life".

Burn's childhood is a tragic story of wandering, rejection and betrayal; in his own words: "I was born in poverty, nursed in sorrow and reared in difficulties, hardships and privations." His father left his mother a few weeks after he was born and he was brought up by his step-father, William McNamee, a drunken ex-soldier who made a precarious living as a pedlar, roaming around Northumberland and the Scottish Lowlands. A violent and emotional man, McNamee was quite capable of cuffing and kissing his step-son within the space of a few minutes; but he did teach him the rudiments of reading and seems to have inspired a genuine affection in the boy.

At 15 Burn was sent to live with his natural father, now settled as a weaver and small-holder in Ireland. It was a hard life and he was scarcely made welcome. But he stuck it out for a year before fleeing back to his mother, only to find that his step-father had died in the meantime and his mother had remarried, making him a "stranger in what should have been a home to me".

Taking to the road, Burn survived on casual labouring jobs. Travelling on foot, he covered immense distances, tramping from Glasgow to London. On one occasion he walked 62 miles in a single day, searching for harvesting work.

Although uneducated, Burn was a keen and intelligent observer of the changes which were transforming Britain before his eyes. Turnpike roads were bringing widely differing individuals and communities into

50 A tramping artisan presents his credentials and finds a warm welcome.

closer contact than ever before. Newspapers, schools and political clubs were creating a better informed public. And modern industry was creating new wealth, even though it was still distributed very unevenly by regions and classes. Everywhere men and women faced not just the possibility but the certainty of change. Coping with change was to become the theme of Burn's life. At the age of 19 Burn became apprenticed to a hatter. Looking back, he saw this step as "the grand turning-point in my existence; to me it was the half-way house between the desert of my youth and the sunny lands of my manhood". An apprenticeship meant the acquisition of a skill, of security and of status – in other words, of the chance to become a respectable working man. As if to seal his new position in society Burn met and married a servant girl, Kitty, within a year of starting his apprenticeship. But it did not mean the end of his nomadic existence, for like many other skilled men of the period, he became a "tramping artisan", travelling from London to Dublin and from Edinburgh to Dorset in his search for work. Burn's horizons broadened in other ways as well; from his mid-twenties onwards he became a voracious reader – "which opened

up to my inquiring mind a rich field of useful knowledge". This knowledge was not "useful" in the sense that it helped him earn more money; but it made him feel like an educated man and a cut above those of his fellows who knew no more of the world than tavern gossip.

In 1830 Burn finally settled in the Glasgow area, where he was to remain for the next 20 years. Four years' steady work gave him enough capital to set up on his own but in 1836 his business began to fail and he gave it up to run a public house. The "Hatters' Arms" lasted for two years before it, too, failed. At this point Burn's world was visibly crumbling around him. In 1837 Kitty had died in a typhus epidemic, leaving him with five children to care for. The youngest, a five-month-old boy, soon followed her, struck down by the same disease.

Burn refused to go under, re-married and tried to set up in business as a hatter again. He could not have picked a worse time. The slump of 1837-42 was the worst to hit Britain for a century. And his own skills as a maker of felt hats were being rendered worthless by a new fashion for silk ones. Abandoning his business again, Burn went back to keeping a public house, moved on to a second, and,

51   Poor man's paradise – a nineteenth-century pub. Notice the child (centre) sent to collect drink in a bottle.

when that too failed, found himself in 1848 a middle-aged man "left without a shilling to commence in the world in some new line". But Burn never blamed the general state of the economy for his plight. Always he saw his failure as a personal one.

If his trade apprenticeship failed to give Burn the prosperous career he longed for, his political apprenticeship did open up a long life of involvement in public affairs. He rapidly graduated from reading radical newspapers to becoming a member of the Glasgow Trades Committee and a member of the central committee of the Glasgow Reform Association. He attended the national delegate meetings of hatters held at Manchester in 1833 and Liverpool in 1834 and joined the Chartists, only to resign after the Chartist convention of 1839 called for a general strike. At that point he turned to the Oddfellows, a skilled workmen's association, which ran a sort of self-help social security system for its members. Once again, Burn rose rapidly through the ranks to play a leading part in establishing a network of branches in his part of Scotland and to be elected to the Board of

Directors itself in 1846. But he resigned after a year and left the movement altogether a few years later, probably because his peronal financial problems made it impossible for him to spare the time for any unpaid activity.

Between 1848 and 1853 Burn passed through another period of extreme insecurity, living variously in Glasgow, York, Leeds, Liverpool, Manchester, Guildford and Hull, and working as a salesman, a book deliverer and a compiler of commercial directories. In 1853 he at last landed what looked like a secure job; ironically for a man whose own enterprises had so often failed, it was as a debt collector. He now had the leisure to write his *Autobiography* and to reflect upon his ultimate good fortune:

The ground that I walked over as a beggar, I have also traversed in the character of a gentleman, and upon more occasions than one, at the houses where I once sought alms, I have been saluted with the respect due to rank far above my own. For the last two years I have held a situation of considerable responsibility, and during that time I have come into contact with many of the first-class commercial men in the United Kingdom.

Alas, it was not to last. Two years later he was broke again after his employer's business failed. He went through difficulties again in 1860 – and again in 1861. Rescue came in the form an invitation and £3 from a son-in-law who had emigrated to America. Burn needed no second telling; but he refused to live off his relatives and went back to his old trade as a hatter. Returning to England in 1865, he first got a job as a journalist on the *Hexham Courant* and then moved to London to become a clerk, first of all in a government office and then at the Crystal Palace. By now he had written three more books, dealing respectively with recent social changes in Britain, social conditions in the U.S.A. and the rights and responsibilities of trade unions. In 1871 Burn took up his final post, as inspector of stores for the Great Eastern Railway in Suffolk. He worked on until 1881 when, his second wife having died, he went to live with a married daughter in Hammersmith – a quiet ending to a very unquiet life.

52 Emigrants waiting to embark at Liverpool, 1850.

Emanuel Lovekin (1820-1905)

My mother was a big strong woman and not cast down with a little thing, but struggled through with a family of seven sons and daughters, with a man that did not seem to take very little interest in home matters. We were all under control of the Mother, who held a masterly hand. (From Lovekin's own account of himself, quoted in *Useful Toil* by J. Burnett)

Emanuel Lovekin, born in 1820 in Tunstall, Staffordshire, probably owed such education as he had to the influence of his mother. But as an education it didn't amount to much:

I was born when schooling was not thought very much of among the poorer people, and there was but very few schools. I never knew but one with a man teacher. There was a few old women's schools. . . . I was sent to an old Lady's school. . . . I cannot remember anything I learned but a song . . .

But it was a Methodist song and Emanuel Lovekin remained a Methodist and a Sunday School teacher for the whole of his long life.

Although small for his age he was sent to work down a coal mine when he was seven and a half. At first he spent the entire day in the dark, opening and closing a trap door for waggons to pass through. Later he was promoted to driving a donkey. At 13 he broke his thigh in an accident at work and had to lie in bed for three months. Long hours of enforced leisure gave him a strong desire to learn to read. Friends who could read came round in the evenings to read aloud to him "and I began to learn a little, and when I was able I went to night School", where he learned to read quite well and to write a little, although his spelling always remained rather shaky. He also went to the Wrockmerdine Primitive Mehodist Sunday School. And, as a result of these efforts, "I was looked up to as something alien to the common class of young men."

When he was about 20 Lovekin found himself falling on hard times, like most other people he knew.

53 A Dame school. Note the variety of ages and lack of facilities.

54 A mass-meeting out in the countryside – beyond the immediate reach of the local J.P.s. Note the slogan "Union is strength".

Little work and very little for it . . . the condition of working people especially, from 1839 to 1842, was very discouraging.

He joined the Chartists and became secretary of his local branch because he could read and write a little. And so he "got mixed up with some of its great men". At first it was exhilarating:

I even thought myself somebody, I felt very earnest in the work I had to do, which was not very small. Meetings almost every night, and now and then very large gatherings. We had one . . . when over 30,000 were there . . .

When the meetings turned to riots, membership of the Chartists became a very different matter. There was a riot not far away and, although he took no part in it, Lovekin was arrested as a prominent local activist in the Chartist movement. He was tried but set free. And that was the effective end of his political activities:

I very probably learned a lesson for my after life. For I was more careful what society I was mixed up in.

But Emanuel Lovekin was still restless and so went off with a friend to work as a railway navvy and a quarryman:

We got some very good jobs and got plenty of money but could not keep it as we did not stop long in one place or at one job.

Returning to his birthplace in 1843, Lovekin married Edna Simcock,

. . . which I never repented the act, but we lived happy together till death parted us in 1881, after being married thirty-six years, having fourteen children, eight boys and six girls.

Not surprisingly, marriage and its responsibilities brought new financial burdens:

It took all I could get to keep myself before I was married. But afterwards I had to keep many more. . . . So I had always plenty of ways to spend what I got.

Lovekin spent most of the rest of his life working as a "butty", a man who hired his own team of miners to open up or manage a mine on behalf of the owner. He knew his job well enough and when the law required it in 1872 got a certificate of professional competence when other men were turned down. But it was by no means a secure living. On one occasion a mine-owner tried to cheat him and he had to take him to court for what he was owed for himself and his men. On another occasion he went into partnership with some friends to open up a new seam but found that the coal was worthless, burnt as hard as brick in an underground fire. The venture cost him £500 and left him in despair:

. . . now I was in a fix. I had lost my money, got a large family and no place. What to do I did not know and it nearly got too much for me to bear. I remember being in a field and scarce knew where I was and what I was doing. I prayed to God to open my way. And I had such a manifestation of God's mercies and goodness, that I felt certain that I should see them all reared . . .

Lovekin's faith was rewarded. Ten of his children survived to have children of their

own. Most lived in the West Midlands, but three emigrated to America, where he visited them twice. Lovekin himself worked on until the age of 79. In 1904 he confessed he was "now very feeble. But still moderate taking all things together". He died the following year.

55 Pit heads in Staffordshire. Notice the small scale of the workings.

56 Mining misery supporting the idle rich – a contemporary comment on inequality.

James Watson (1795-1874)

While men as highly placed as Lord Shaftesbury and as humble as Emanuel Lovekin found in their Christian faith the mainspring of their lives, others dedicated themselves to opposing the influence of conventional religion. One such was James Watson.

Watson was born in 1795 in the small town of Malton in Yorkshire and was left fatherless when less than a year old. His mother, a Sunday School teacher, saw that he had some schooling and, when he was 12, got him a position in a clergyman's house as a general help – working in the garden, caring for the horses, milking the cows and waiting at table.

At the age of 18 Watson went off to Leeds, a booming industrial city, and found another job, also caring for horses. And it was there that he first came into contact with a group of "radical reformers" who met together to read opposition papers such as William Cobbett's *Register* and Richard Carlile's *Republican*. Within a short time Watson had become a "freethinker", a person who did not accept conventional Christian beliefs. Some freethinkers still believed in God. Others made a religion out of Nature or a vague belief in progress. Others were outright atheists.

At that time the freethinking Richard Carlile (1790-1843) was in Dorchester prison for publishing what the government considered to be blasphemous literature. Watson not only sold this literature in Leeds but also collected money to help Carlile and agreed to go to London to keep his shop open. In due course he was himself arrested and sentenced to a year in prison. It was not such a terrible fate. The gaoler was a kindly man and Watson spent most of his time reading history and "freethinking" works or conversing with another well-educated prisoner. In many ways this period of confinement helped to make up for the shortcomings of his own early education.

When Watson tried to look for other work

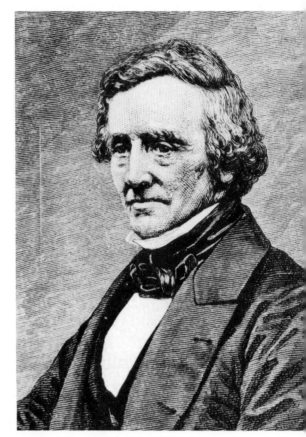

57 James Watson, radical.

after his release he found the outside world somewhat harsher than his captivity:

I . . . found my having been in prison and shopman to Mr. Carlile a formidable difficulty and I incurred in consequence considerable privation.

So Watson returned to Carlile's shop because he had nowhere else to go and continued to run it for him until he was released in 1825. In that year Watson mastered a new skill – printing – and encountered a new outlook on the world – Owenism. And so

. . . to the end of 1829 I was actively engaged

UNITED

TO **PROTECT.**

NOT COMBINED TO INJURE.

To the Operative of the Grand National Consolidated TRADES UNION of Great Britain and Ireland.

WE, the undersigned Officers of the GRAND LODGE of *Operative* duly incorporated with the GRAND NATIONAL CONSOLIDATED TRADES UNION OF GREAT BRITAIN AND IRELAND, do hereby grant unto and to this Dispensation, authorizing them to institute and form, under this our Order, a LODGE, of *Operative* at the House of in the of in the County of for the purpose of enabling the *Operative* of that District more effectually to watch over and protect the INTERESTS of their TRADE, to establish the Rights of Industry, secure the Blessings of Prosperity, and for the purpose of affording them the means of promoting General Knowledge, Good Habits, Social Friendship, Peace, Harmony, and Brotherly Love amongst them, and to aid them in giving Mutual Protection, Consolation, and Assistance to each other in the time of Oppression, Affliction, or Need.

Provided always that the Officers and Members of such Lodge do strictly conform to all and every of the Articles and Regulations of the *National Consolidated Trades' Union* aforesaid, and so long as they do not wilfully disturb the public peace by violating the Laws of these Realms.

Given under our Hand and Seal, this Day of One Thousand, Eight Hundred, and Thirty-Four.

Grand Master,

Deputy Grand Master,

Grand Secretary.

58 Authorization to establish a branch of the G.N.C.T.U.

with others in forming societies for political and religious liberty, co-operative associations etc.

He also managed a co-operative store and in 1830 went back to tour around his native Yorkshire and encourage local people to form their own co-operative stores.

Returning to London, Watson opened a bookshop and in 1831 branched out to become a printer and publisher as well. He also became a keen member of the National Union of the Working Classes. In 1832 cholera struck Britain and the government ordered one day to be set aside for a "general fast" as a way of pleading for divine intervention. The National Union of the Working Classes' members "to mark their contempt for such an order, determined to have a procession through the streets of London, and afterwards to have a general feast". Watson was arrested for organizing and leading the procession and, after conducting his own defence, was acquitted of any crime.

In 1833 Watson was convicted of selling the *Poor Man's Guardian*, a radical publication which defied the law by refusing to pay the government's tax on newspapers, because it was intended to deny poor men knowledge of current affairs. Watson served another prison sentence, this time for six months. Unrepentant, he joined a meeting to celebrate

59 A London bookshop of the mid-nineteenth century.

60 Chartist petition carried to Parliament 1842. Notice the slogans on the flags "Reform", "More Pigs and Less Parson", "Universal Suffrage", "Liberty", "Vote by Ballot".

the third anniversary of the French revolution of 1830 on the very day that he was released. The following year he attended the immense trade union protest meeting organized on behalf of the "Tolpuddle Martyrs".

Shortly after his marriage in 1835 Watson was imprisoned again for a further six months. Unshaken, he joined the Chartists on his release and was one of the six working men who joined six M.P.s in a committee to draw up the six points of the "People's Charter". Even before the collapse of Chartism, however, Watson had switched his main allegiance to free-thinking and Owenism, joining G. J. Holyoake to publish the *Reasoner* from 1846 onwards. In 1853 Watson became President of the newly formed London Secular Society. In 1854 he announced his retirement as a publisher and moved to be near the re-sited Crystal Palace so that he could spend his old age visiting its exhibitions and listening to concerts. But he retained an interest in politics and was a strong sympathizer with the republican uprising in Poland in 1863. His last public duty was to attend a final gathering of Owenites in 1871. He died in 1874 after a long illness.

The causes Watson championed – radical politics and freethinking – were either repulsive or incomprehensible to most of his countrymen. But he insisted:

I have had but one object in view – to show my fellow-workmen that the humblest amongst them may render effectual aid to the cause of progress.

Of course, that was a view that even Shaftesbury might have endorsed. Victorians of widely differing political and religious views believed in the desirability of "progress"; where they differed was in their definitions of what it was and how it was to be achieved.

GLOSSARY

Anti Corn Law League Organization established in Manchester in 1839, and led by Richard Cobden (1804-65) and John Bright (1811-89), to campaign against the Corn Laws (*see below*) and in favour of Free Trade policies, using mass meetings and other propaganda techniques. It drew much support from the manufacturing interest and middle-classes, whose growing political importance it represented. It was disbanded after the abolition of the Corn Laws in 1846.

Blanketeers, March of the (1817) Abortive attempt by Lancashire textile workers, suffering from post-war unemployment to march on London and petition for relief. Equipped with blankets for nights in the open they were dispersed by the military by the time they reached Derbyshire. 200 were arrested.

Catholic emancipation Legislation finally passed by Parliament in 1829 to extend to Roman Catholics almost the same civil and political rights enjoyed by members of the Church of England.

Cato Street Conspiracy (1820) Plot, led by Arthur Thistlewood, to assassinate the Cabinet and set up a revolutionary government. Most of the plotters were seized at their Cato Street headquarters. Five were hanged and five transported for life. An extreme movement, outside the mainstream of radical protest, it seemed to justify the Six Acts (*see below*).

Chartism Working-class mass-movement arising out of the economic depression after 1836 and united by support for the People's Charter, drawn up in 1838, which demanded a more democratic constitution by means of annual parliaments, adult male suffrage, payment of M.P.s, abolition of the property qualification for M.P.s, equal constituencies and the secret ballot. A national convention (1839) failed to agree on a national strike but presented a massive petition to Parliament, which rejected it, and a second one in 1842. Ineffectual but widespread strikes and riots followed and the movement fizzled out after a third attempt at petitioning Parliament inspired by the continental revolutions of 1848. Its supporters were perhaps too diverse in their ultimate social objectives to enable the movement to succeed but it did show that the working class could organize on a massive scale and provided many radicals and union leaders with their political apprenticeship.

Combination Acts Legislation passed in 1799 and 1800 to prohibit the formation of trade unions and substantially repealed in 1824.

Corn Laws Legislation passed in 1815 and 1828 to regulate imports of grain in an attempt to protect British agricultural investments. The system failed to achieve this objective and opened the way to price-rigging by speculators. The Corn Laws antagonized both urban workers and the manufacturing interest and became a hated symbol of aristocratic privilege, vilified by the orators of the Anti Corn Law League. The abolition of the Corn Laws in 1846, following the Irish famine of 1845, split the Tory party for a generation.

Evangelicals Members of the Church of England strongly committed to spreading the gospel at home and abroad and applying Christian principles to daily life and political issues. Emphasizing preaching and Bible-reading rather than elaborate acts of worship, they supported many humanitarian reforms; but their main concern was individual salvation through unbending faith in the truth of the Christian message.

Factory Acts Legislation passed to regulate working conditions, at first only in the textiles industries, by limiting the hours of work and ages of employees and imposing elementary standards of safety. Sir Robert Peel Senior's Health and Morals of Apprentices Act marked the way forward in 1802 but the turning-point came in 1833 when the Act passed in that year provided for independent inspectors, rather than J.P.s, to enforce its provisions. Subsequent legislation imposed tighter regulations and extended them to a wider range of employments.

Great Exhibition (1851) The brain-child of Albert, Prince Consort, this international exhibition of arts and manufacturers attracted six million visitors to its Hyde Park site and demonstrated to the world Britain's technological superiority and cultural self-confidence. The profits helped to establish the South Kensington museum complex.

Hungry Forties An American financial crisis in 1836 and the ending of the first railway-building boom led to a period of unemployment and protest which gave rise to Chartism and the Anti Corn Law League (*see above*). Trade recovery and a new burst of railway-building saw a general improvement in economic conditions after 1842.

Laissez-faire Belief that government activities, regulations and taxes should be kept to a minimum to enable private citizens to pursue their own interests as they wished. *Laissez-faire* theories received their classic statement in Adam Smith's *The Wealth of Nations* (1776), which eventually inspired Peel's Free Trade budgets (1842-6). But at the same time urban and industrial problems were forcing governments to take on new responsibilities for protecting private citizens from the evil effects of their actions on each other.

Luddism Working-class protest movement aimed at opposing the spread of new textile machines which threatened traditional methods and standards of workmanship and increased fears of unemployment. Machine-wreckers, supposedly led by a "King Ludd" or "Ned Ludd", were especially active in the North and Midlands in the years 1811-17.

Mechanics' Institute Education organization established by George Birkbeck (1776-1841) in 1822 to provide basic and technical education to working men by means of evening classes. By 1850 there were over 700 such institutes.

Mines Act (1842) Legislation passed as a result of Parliamentary enquiry which exposed exploitative and unhealthy conditions in the mines. The Act forbade females to work underground and limited the hours and ages of male workers. Later Acts improved standards of safety inspection.

New Poor Law Method of poor relief established in 1834 largely as a reaction against the Speenhamland system which was regarded as wasteful and an unjustified interference with the free operation of the labour market. Henceforth relief was only to be granted to able-bodied paupers if they resided in workhouses under strict regulations and accepted a standard of living deliberately set below anything an employed person could provide for himself. The New Poor Law claimed the virtues of cheapness and efficiency but was seen as heartless and provoked widespread public resistance, especially in the North. Its harshness was curbed after the Andover scandal of 1847.

Peterloo (1819) Mass-meeting of 80,000 in favour of parliamentary reform held at St Peter's Fields, Manchester. Magistrates, alarmed at the size of the crowd, ordered the arrest of "Orator" Hunt, the main speaker. Inexperienced yeomanry executing this order killed 11 and wounded 400. Their inglorious intervention contrasted grotesquely with recent national pride in the victory at Waterloo – hence the nickname for the incident, which helped to panic the government into passing the Six Acts (*see below*).

Radical Term loosely applied to any person or group committed to seeking fundamental reforms, basically in politics, but also in the Church, education, etc. In the early nineteenth century the term was especially applied to supporters of parliamentary reform, who saw a reformed parliament as the necessary instrument through which further changes could be implemented.

Six Acts (1819) Legislation passed after Peterloo (*see above*) limiting freedom of assembly to 50 persons (without flags or banners), prohibiting military drilling, and empowering J.P.s to search houses for suspected weapons or pamphlets.

Speenhamland System System of poor relief devised by Berkshire magistrates, meeting at Speenhamland in 1795 after a run of three bad harvests had led to general distress among the poor of the county. Payments were made to men according to the size of their families and the price of bread. The system was widely copied in the rural South and East but had the long-term effect of depressing wages and tying men to the locality in which they were entitled to claim relief. It also trebled the cost of the Poor Law by 1812. It was abolished by the New Poor Law of 1834.

"Swing" "Captain Swing" was the alleged organizer of a widespread outbreak of rural protest in southern and eastern England in 1830-1. The smashing of threshing-machines and the burning of ricks and barns was met with equal ferocity by the rural gentry. 19 men were hanged, 481 transported and 644 imprisoned.

Ten Hours Act (1847) Legislation passed after a sustained (1831-47) campaign to limit the normal working day for women and children in factories to ten hours. As their labour was essential to men the hope was that their hours would be effectively limited to ten as well. But shift labour defeated this aim until 1874 when a ten-hour norm was finally established by law.

Tolpuddle Martyrs The attempt by six agricultural labourers at Tolpuddle, Dorset, to form a trade union branch in 1834 led to their prosecution for administering unlawful oaths. Sentenced to seven years' transportation, they became the object of widespread organized sympathy and were released after two years. Five went to Canada and one came home.

Transportation System of punishment (1788-1867) by which convicted criminals and political dissidents were taken to serve out their seven-year, 14-year or life sentences in penal servitude in Australia, where they worked on farms or built roads or other public facilities. Few of the 160,000 transported ever returned to Britain.

DATE LIST

1815 Battle of Waterloo, Corn Laws passed.
1816 Cobbett's "Twopenny Trash". Robert Owen's Infant School.
1817 March of the Blanketeers. Habeas Corpus suspended.
1819 Peterloo Six Acts.
1820 Cato St Conspiracy.
1821 First Channel steamer service begins.
1823 Stephensons open world's first locomotive works.
1824 Repeal of the Combination Acts.
1825 Opening of the Stockton & Darlington Railway.
1826 Richard Carlile sells first ever birth-control manual.
1828 Britain's first zoo opens in Regent's Park.
1829 Catholic Emancipation, Metropolitan Police established.
1830 Swing riots. Liverpool & Manchester Railway opened.

1831 Reform riots in Nottingham, Derby and Bristol.
1832 Reform Bill passed.
1833 Factory Act. First state grant for education.
1834 New Poor Law.
1836 Registration of births, deaths and marriages.
1837 Electric Telegraph invented.
1838 Brunel's *Great Western*
1839 Anti-Corn Law League established.
1840 Penny Post introduced.
1842 Mines Act. Chadwick's Report. Chartist demonstration.
1843 First Christmas cards introduced.
1845 Irish famine.
1846 Repeal of the Corn Laws.
1847 Ten Hours Act.
1848 Public Health Act.
1849 First electric street lighting in Britain.
1851 Great Exhibition.

BIOGRAPHICAL NOTES

Albert, Prince Consort (1819-61). A cultured German prince whose marriage to Victoria in 1840 brought her a large family, 20 years of domestic bliss and 40 of inconsolable grief after his sudden death from typhoid. Mastermind of the Great Exhibition of 1851, he also popularized two lasting Victorian institutions – Christmas trees and holidays in Scotland – and also did his best to teach Victoria how to be a constitutional ruler.

Bagehot, Walter (1826-77). Writer, journalist and man of affairs, educated at University College, London. Editor of *The Economist* and author of *The English Constitution* and *Lombard St*, which explained respectively the realities of British politics and the City.

Bentham, Jeremy (1748-1832) Philosopher and legal reformer, usually recognized as the central figure of the "Utilitarian" movement, which attacked unthinking attachment to tradition and corrupt institutions. Founder of the *Westminster Review* and of University College, London, and one of the few British thinkers to achieve a worldwide reputation in his own life-time.

Birkbeck, George (1776-1841). Founder, with Bentham, Brougham and Cobbett, of the London Mechanics' Institute (1824) which held evening classes to help working men catch up on the education they had missed. Birkbeck College, University of London today continues this tradition of part-time study.

Bright, John (1811-89). Liberal M.P. (1843-89) and leading spokesman of the "Manchester School" of political economy which advocated free trade as the best path to national prosperity. A passionate opponent of aggressive foreign action such as the Crimean War.

Brontë, Charlotte (1816-55). Author of *Jane Eyre*; died in childbirth.

Brougham, Henry (1778-1868). Lawyer, reformer and collaborator with Bentham in founding University College. Played a leading role in the passage of the 1832 Reform Act.

Carlyle, Thomas (1795-1881). Critic and essayist, chiefly remembered for *The French Revolution* (1837) and the theory that hero figures are the movers of history.

Cobden, Richard (1804-65). Liberal M.P. (1841-65) and collaborator with John Bright. Chief negotiator of the 1860 trade treaty with France which bears his name.

Dickens, Charles (1812-70). Journalist and novelist whose social criticism awoke the middle classes to the contemporary evils of the Poor Law, private education, the corruption of the legal system and the destructive effects of greed and ambition.

Disraeli, Benjamin (1809-81). Speculator, best-selling novelist, traveller and supreme political tactician who hi-jacked the wreckage of the Tory party after its split over the Corn Laws and turned it into the modern Conservative party.

Eliot, George (1819-80). Pen name of Mary Ann Evans, author of *Silas Marner* and *Middlemarch*.

Fry, Elizabeth (1780-1845). Norwich-born Quaker who awoke to seriousness when visiting Newgate and devoted her life to prison reform, achieving a European reputation, while simultaneously raising a large family.

George III, (1738-1820). "I glory in the name of Briton" said the ruler who died, in Shelley's words, "an old, mad, blind, despised king". A model husband and father, and a talented amateur at farming and music, he was genuinely popular with the common people but from 1788 his life was clouded by the effects of porphyria, an hereditary blood disease which robbed him of his wits and exposed him to cruel treatment at the hands of uncomprehending doctors.

George IV, (1762-1830). Regent from 1811 and king from 1820, this vain, spendthrift and unloved connoisseur gave his title to an era and a style as extravagant as himself. His fabulous Pavilion at Brighton has been called the "most fantastic palace in Europe" – and rightly so.

Kingsley, Charles (1819-79). Chaplain to Queen Victoria, advocate of Christian socialism and author of such popular novels as *The Water Babies* and *Westward Ho!*.

Lancaster, Joseph (1778-1838). Educationist and advocate of the "monitorial system" by which chosen assistants relayed the teacher's instruction to the mass of pupils, supposedly a cheap method of "mass-producing" knowledge.

Liverpool, Lord (1770-1828). Tory Prime Minister (1812-27) whose period of office was marked by reactionary and repressive policies such as the widespread use of spies and the Six Acts which suspended civil liberties.

Maudslay, Henry (1771-1831). Mechanical engineer and inventor of the metal lathe and the slide rule.

Mill, John Stuart (1806-73). Philosopher, economist and heir to Bentham as the leading "Utilitarian", though a much more subtle one. In his later years he became a champion of socialism and women's rights.

Newman, John Henry, Cardinal (1801-90). Anglican thinker and leader of the "Oxford Movement", who converted in 1846 to become a leader of the Catholic revival in England.

Nightingale, Florence (1820-1910). Founder of the modern profession of nursing.

Paine, Tom (1737-1809). Radical pamphleteer who played a leading role in both the American and French revolutions. His direct, vigorous prose introduced generations of British workers to democratic and anti-clerical ideas.

Peel, Sir Robert (1778-1850). Tory Prime Minister (1834-5 and 1841-6), chiefly remembered for the establishment of the Metropolitan Police (1829), Catholic Emancipation (1829), a series of tariff-reducing budgets (1841-5) and the repeal of the Corn Laws (1846).

Telford, Thomas (1747-1834). Founder of the modern civil engineering profession and builder of the suspension bridge over the Menai Strait, St Katherine's Dock, London and the Caledonian Canal.

William IV (1765-1837). King whose unspectacular naval career was followed by an unspectacular royal one – a real achievement in turbulent times.

BOOKS FOR FURTHER READING

General Background
Asa Briggs, *Victorian People* (Penguin)
Asa Briggs, *The Age of Improvement* (Longmans)
G. Kitson Clark, *The Making of Victorian England* (Methuen)
G.D.H. Cole and A.W. Filson, *British Working Class Movements: Select Documents 1789-1870* (Macmillan)
J.F.C. Harrison, *Early Victorian Britain* (Fontana)
Dorothy Marshall, *Industrial England 1776-1851* (Routledge & Kegan Paul)
Richard Tames, *Economy & Society in Nineteenth-Century Britain* (Allen & Unwin)

General Biographies
John Burnett, *Useful Toil* (Penguin)
Richard Tames, *Makers of Modern Britain* (Batsford)

Biographies of Individuals
John Pudney, *Brunel & His World* (Thames & Hudson)
Richard Tames, *Isambard Kingdom Brunel* (Shire)
David Vincent, *The Autobiography of a Beggar Boy* (James Dawson Burn) (Europe)
Roger Watson, *Edwin Chadwick, Poor Law and Public Health* (Longman)
Asa Briggs, *William Cobbett* (Oxford University Press)
Raymond Williams, *William Cobbett* (Fontana)
J.F.C. Harrison, *Robert Owen & the Owenites in Britain & America*
John Anthony, *Joseph Paxton* (Shire)
Michael Robbins, *George & Robert Stephenson* (Oxford University Press)
Amoret & Christopher Scott, *Wellington* (Shire)

INDEX